Cuthbert Bede

The Curate of Cranston

With other prose and verse

Cuthbert Bede

The Curate of Cranston
With other prose and verse

ISBN/EAN: 9783337075644

Printed in Europe, USA, Canada, Australia, Japan

Cover: Foto ©Thomas Meinert / pixelio.de

More available books at **www.hansebooks.com**

THE

Curate of Cranston;

WITH

Other Prose and Verse.

BY

CUTHBERT BEDE,

AUTHOR OF "MR. VERDANT GREEN," "GLENCREGGAN," ETC., ETC.

LONDON:

SAUNDERS, OTLEY, AND CO.,

66, BROOK STREET, HANOVER SQUARE.

1862.

TO THE READER.

THE Tales of "The Curate of Cranston" and "Mareli," together with some other pieces, are here printed
for the first time. The remaining Prose and Verse
articles have appeared, during the last fifteen years, in
the publications indicated in the following Table of
Contents.

CONTENTS.

viii   *Contents.*

THE

CURATE OF CRANSTON,

ETC., ETC.

CHAPTER I.

CRANSTON AND ITS INHABITANTS.

You would more readily have found Cranston in the
county map, than in the county itself. It was a
leading peculiarity of its situation that it was eight
miles distant from everywhere—from every town, at
least, that aspired to the dignity of holding a market,
and electing its own mayor and corporation. But,
although it was the centre of a system of towns, the
roads in and around Cranston were in so decided a
state of nature, that the parish was virtually cut off
from all connection with the outer world, except in
one direction, where the accident of a road that, by
Cranston courtesy, might be called tolerably good,
had decided the Cranston people in the selection of
Closeborough as their peculiar metropolis. Their
connection with Closeborough was certainly not of

B

an over-intimate kind; for it was limited to one day
in the week. This was on the Saturdays, when the
Cranston farmers drove to Closeborough in that
singular species of vehicle which Sydney Smith
called the "pre-adamite buggy," and there munched
wheat out of little bags that might have been the
money-bags from the bank of Nature; and felt beasts
in those portions of their anatomy which were destined to be covered with fat; and discussed the merits
of "this here ship," and "that there ship," as though
they had been British sailors instead of Cranston
sheep-farmers; and in bar-parlours and over glasses
of heady ale and fiery brandy-and-water, talked about
mangles, and wuts, and stock, and the rise and fall
of markets, and the shortcomings of landlords, and
the outgoings of business, until it was time for them
to drive their farmeresses back to Cranston.   On these
occasions, they carried off the Closeborough penny
paper, which supplied them daily with homœopathic
doses of literary food, until the Saturday again came
round.

In addition to the pre-adamite buggies, and a
donkey that dragged its cart along as slowly as though
it were a needless Alexandrine, there was an indigenous
carrier, of a hopefully-speculative turn of mind, who,
every Saturday, undertook the overland route to

Closeborough, and obtained the fitful patronage of the
Cranston population **in the matter of** butter, **eggs,**
and poultry. With the exception of that slight flut-
tering towards intellectual activity which may have
been occasioned by an attentive perusal of the Closeborough penny paper, the Cranston mind remained
in a dormant state, from the close of one Saturday
to the dawn of another; **but on** market days it was
roused from its customary lethargy, and, for a **few**
hours of unwonted bustle and **noise, opened its eyes**
and ears to the varied sights and **sounds with which**
on all sides it was **deafened** and bewildered. **While**
the masculine **mind of Cranston was surrendered to**
agricultural matters, and the contemplation of new
scarifiers and steam-cultivators, **the feminine intellect**
was chiefly devoted **to** the drapery establishments,
with their decided bargains and fashionable novelties
in bonnet-ribbons and flowers for cap-borders. The
enervating effect produced upon **the** Cranston mind,
both male and female, by this strain upon its intellectual faculties, was evidenced, **not only by** the majority
of the male Cranstonians leaving Closeborough in
that fuddled state locally known as " market peert,"
but also by the general lassitude displayed on the following day by those who attended the services at
Cranston Church.

It was not that the Curate was dull in his preaching, or low in his delivery; for, **on** the contrary, the Rev. Hugh Raymond had a voice that could be heard by the aged and half-deaf; and he not only read the prayers distinctly and impressively, but he also preached a plain and not too-long sermon, in a tongue that could be "understanded of the people." It clearly **was not the** Curate's fault if the majority of his congregation deliberately closed their eyes, as a preparatory measure to nodding their heads, whenever they sat down, whether their session was short or long, or during the lessons, prayers, or sermon. Their somnolence had become a fixed habit, and, because it was a pleasant one, was not to be abandoned at the mere suggestion of a stranger. For, the Curate frequently admonished them on this subject in private and friendly visits; and sometimes would pleasantly say to them, "I hope you will have a better night's rest to-night than you could have had last Saturday night; or else you may sleep as much over your work to-morrow, as you did during the service last Sunday morning." But pleasantries were lost on people who were incapable of seeing the point of a joke, unless it was of a breadth and calibre equivalent to the "Facetiæ" and American anecdotes weekly printed for their special amusement in a certain column of the Closeborough penny paper; and admonitions, however kind **and** forcible, were of no avail in breaking through **a** custom on which the Cranston mind had fastened with tenacious perseverance many a long year before Hugh Raymond had set foot in the parish. If he could have kept his congregation standing through the service, or if he could have changed the market-day from the Saturday to the Monday, he might have **had** a chance of preaching to people who opened their **eyes,** if not their hearts and minds. But, as it was, the excitement of the Closeborough market-day was probably too much for them, and the reaction on the morrow was in keeping with the local characteristics of the parish.

For, Cranston was a sort of sleepy hollow; a spot whose physical features had apparently infected the people with a kindred dulness. From the force of circumstances, it seemed as though a drowsy sluggish**ess** of intellect was indigenous to the tillers of the Cranston soil; and with whatever fork the Curate might endeavour to expel this dulness of their nature, nevertheless it would return. It was a down-looking, poverty-stricken, ague-loving place, lying in a swampy valley where rheumatism held its sway, and into which the agricultural enlightenment of deep draining had not yet penetrated. It was the centre of a labyrinth of narrow

rutty lanes that wound their devious courses between
tall banks and hedge-rows, and were muddy even in a
summer's drought.   **A wide stretch** of open common
extended from Cranston in an easterly direction, and
afforded but very scanty pasturage to the sheep and
cattle that were condemned to seek their livelihood
amid its rushy bogs; and, on the far side of the com-
mon was an outlying hamlet of the parish of Cranston—a hamlet which had been lying out for so long a
time **in** this desolate region that **its air** of mingled
melancholy **and wildness was not to be** wondered at.
Here, in the very midst of the bleak bare landscape, **a**
few miserable cottages were huddled together as though
for friendly warmth and fellowship.

Down in Cranston itself, the houses were dotted
about irregularly, chiefly in detachments of twos **and**
threes, with, here and there, an attenuated farm-house,
in keeping with the poverty of the district; and over
everything was an air of damp, decay, and mildew.
In the very centre of the swampy hollow, was the
Church.   It dated from early Norman days, and, after
flourishing for many centuries, had begun to give way before the storms of time, when, in **its** utter helplessness,
it had been compelled to endure sad indignities at the
hands of iconoclastic churchwardens; and it now presented such a heterogeneous mass of Norman mouldings,

sash windows, wooden mullions, brick buttresses, high pews, and omnipresent whitewash, that if ever such an out-of-the-way place had been visited by an architectural and ecclesiological society, its members would have been disposed to assume complimentary mourning for the ruthless destruction of what had once been so perfect and beautiful.

Such was the church and the parish to which Hugh Raymond had devoted those four important years of his life, which closed with his thirtieth birthday. He had flung himself into his work with an energy that had outlived rheumatic fevers, and was neither to be subdued by damp and mildew, nor the coldness of the place and people. No clergyman had hitherto lived among them; there was no resident squire or farmers of the better class,—and the poorer sort of Cranston, comprising, indeed, the whole of the parishioners, had been allowed to lie undisturbed in their swampy hollow for so long a time, that their sluggish natures seemed to resent any benevolent efforts to stir them up to a little warmer life and feeling. Indeed, they appeared to regard the Curate's well-meant exertions to bring about something like a reciprocity of friendship, as an interference on that gentleman's part which could only be overlooked from the consideration that it was his trade, and that he was paid for doing it. If they went to sleep in their high pews with tolerable frequency, and were punctual in their payments to the clothing and coal clubs that Hugh Raymond had established for their benefit—and of which, for the first year, they entertained an idea that the deposits were converted to his own purposes —they considered that they had fulfilled their duties to their parson, and that more could not be reasonably expected of them.

But, unfortunately for the Curate's serenity of mind, he expected more. He had brought to his sacred calling all the depth and strength of his nature. His was a naturally fervid temperament, that made him dissatisfied unless he could perceive some outward show of that friendly sentiment towards him which he daily endeavoured to draw forth ; and, above all, some slight evidence of that improved state of religious feeling which he laboured so zealously to kindle in their breasts. Week after week, and month after month, he smote upon those stony rocks without one responsive gush—not such, at least, as he looked for. But he had the highest motives to incite him to perseverance in his apparently thankless duties; and he was not to be overcome by present discouragement. His was the task to sow the seed in the field that had been appointed to him, whether it was cast on stones

or amid thorns : **and he waited hopefully for the fruit-**
ful evidences **of that which may have been sown**
upon the good **ground.**

CHAPTER II.

CRANSTON'S CURATE AND HIS BELONGINGS.

WHENEVER the Curate of Cranston felt himself **over-**
come **by the melancholy miasma of the place, and**
sorely inclined to think within himself, " **How much**
longer must **my health** and strength be expended on
those **who** heed not the **outlay,** and seem **none the**
better **for it ?** How much longer must I remain in a
parish where I am cut off from so much that is congenial to my tastes ?" — whenever despondency induced him to soliloquize **after this fashion, then there**
would come the thought of his widowed mother, and
he would beat down his dispiriting **fancies, and say,**
" **Here** is my lot; my path is clearly marked **out for**
me ; let me **only strive to walk in** it cheerfully, **and to**
do my duty to God **and man."** And that same day,
perhaps, he would send such **a** letter home to the distant county, where, with her niece, his mother lived
in humble retirement, that the widow's eyes would

swim with tears of joy, and she would say to her companion, "Oh, Margaret! **what a** comfort it is to **think that dear Hugh is so happy."** Margaret **may have had reasons of her own** for knowing the truth of **the matter; but,** whatever her reasons were, she did **not impart them to her aunt,** whose imaginary pictures of Cranston and its inhabitants were as far different **to the** dull **realities sketched in the** preceding chapter, **as many of the works of Turner's** rainbow pencil were to the scenes which they professed to depict.

Yes: **in** that widowed mother's home lay the **chief** reason for Hugh Raymond's **four years' servitude** at Cranston. It was a curacy of **one hundred and eight pounds** a-year!—almost as much as many a skilled mechanic could **obtain**!—and if he were to resign it, he might wait for many years ere he could light upon such another windfall. Most fortunate, indeed, had he accounted himself to be able to obtain it,—a blessing to be acknowledged thankfully and humbly in private prayer, and on bended knee; and very grateful was he **to** his father's old college friend, Sir Marmaduke Wrighton, for having recommended him to his present rector. True it was that the rector—being non-resident and the inhabitants of Cranston being over a certain number—was obliged to pay that large sum to his curate, according to the census of souls; but this was so much the better for the Curate, who took all the duties and the entire responsibility of the parish; for, otherwise, he might have had to do nearly as much work for far less money. So it was a mutual benefit. The Curate received an unusually large stipend, and the rector was enabled to live (for his wife's health, of course,) in a distant parish, whose scenery and society were more attractive than the persons and places in and around Cranston, and only came to Hugh Raymond's parish on tithe-days, for the purpose of carrying off the five hundred and odd pounds that formed his share of the proceeds of the living.

On these half-yearly occasions, the curate received his rector's cheque for fifty-four pounds; and, for four-and-twenty hours, at least, could feel himself a man of capital; though the pleasure was somewhat alloyed by the fear lest this sum (which was the representative of so many necessaries and comforts for his mother and cousin) should make itself wings and flee away before he could take that weary eight-mile walk, and lodge it in the Closeborough Bank. There was always a great mixture of pride and humility about this transaction; pride in having a banking account and a cheque-book, humility in the sum deposited being so small, and drawn out so speedily, that the ac-

cumulated interest would seldom have exceeded five
shillings. When the Curate drew out ten pounds for
his immediate wants, and was asked how he would
have it, "In gold or notes?" there was a peculiar
humility in his invariable reply, "A pound's worth
of silver, and nine sovereigns—if you can spare them."
And the grey-headed clerk, interrupted in his task of
tying up five hundred sovereigns in a bag, would
smile grimly as he replied, "I think we can spare
them;" and would dribble them from a great copper
scoop that shovelled out pecks of sovereigns and half-
sovereigns as though they had been of no more value
than peas and beans.

If the Curate of Cranston occasionally desponded
when he reflected upon his solitary lot, and the lack of
congenial society, he would soon console himself by
the thought that, in his present course of life, he was
saving money for his mother and cousin. If he had
been obliged to mix much in society, it would have entailed upon him many expenses that he was now able
to avoid. And if his curacy had been in a town
or city, he would not only have been compelled to sub-
scribe to all the local charities, but would have been
looked upon by every needy person as their specially-
appointed **almoner;** every beggar's hand would have
been against him, and his own hand would have been

continually in his pocket, as the saying is; though, unlike the charity of many people, which takes their hand to their **pocket only to leave it there,** the Curate would have **drawn forth his closed** upon a piece of money, which would be transferred to the person who had traded upon his sympathy. In a town, too, he would have been constrained to live in more expensive lodgings than those two small, **low** rooms in the cottage at **Cranston, which he found to be** quite large and lofty enough for **all his immediate** needs.

Besides the present **support of his mother and** cousin, — **or rather, of** his mother, for his cousin **earned her** own livelihood,—Hugh Raymond had another motive for economy, and for endeavouring to accumulate in the Closeborough Bank that little store which, originally dwarfed in its dimension, had obstinately refused to grow to any respectable **bulk.** It was a motive based upon a very good **foundation, and** a very pretty one too, for Margaret was **both** pretty and good; and, indeed, that motive was no other than Margaret herself. Hugh Raymond was in the painful condition of a lover who desires to be married, and does not possess a sufficiency of income to justify him in putting an end to his bachelor existence. By dint of the severest economy, after providing for his mother and himself, he could barely save **a** five-pound note each year for his matrimonial fund; and as his mother assured him, from her own experience, that four five-pound notes were not sufficient to start a newly-married couple in furniture and house-keeping, Hugh and Margaret were compelled to rest content with the delightful fact that they were " engaged," and to wait for that problematical " some time or other," when he could place the little hoop of gold upon her finger. It was one **of** those desperate engagements which are **so frequently waged in the battle** of life, in which it is well for **the combatants** if they only lose their hearts, and not their health, **spirits,** and temper. Sometimes everything is lost on either side, and the engagement is equally as devastating as **was the** annihilating strife between the two celebrated cats of Kilkenny.

Hugh's and Margaret's engagement came about in this way. Margaret's mother had died when her firstborn was a mere baby, and Margaret had been brought up by **her aunt** Raymond, who had one other child besides Hugh, a daughter **who only** lived to be ten years **old.** At her death, Mrs. Raymond considered Margaret to possess a still stronger claim upon her as the child of her adoption; and when, a few years after this, Margaret lost her father, the bond between herself **and aunt was** indissolubly strengthened. Indeed, the child had been left by her spendthrift father entirely dependent upon her relatives; and as in this case the affections of kindred are apt to be frozen up, poor Margaret might have been condemned to a long winter of privations and distress, had not her aunt's love changed her young life into a long summer's day. In Mr. Raymond's pleasant country rectory, Margaret and Hugh passed their childhood in those mutual plays and friendly fights that so agreeably diversify the otherwise monotonous existence of extreme youth. Hugh, the senior by five years of his little cousin Maggie, loved to teach her and his sister all the boyish knowledge that his advanced experience enabled him to impart. Through him they were familiar with wasps' nests and rat-holes, and were inducted to the mysteries of manufacturing sailing vessels and gunpowder squibs—exploits and acquirements in which they encountered many mishaps, and by which their bumps of wonder and destructiveness must have been considerably enlarged.

His sister died when Hugh was sent to his first school; and during the holidays he had no one to console him and to play with him except Maggie. Henceforth his cousin took the place of his sister; and it was not until long after he had begun to shave, that he viewed her in any other than a sororial light.

When he went to college, that slight "change came o'er the spirit of his dream," which might by-and-by lead to an awakening in which he would recognize Margaret in a nearer and dearer position than even that of cousin or sister. This change, however, was stealing over him insensibly; and, as yet, he was unconscious of the full advance it had made.

It was not a very rich living that was held by Hugh's father; and Mr. Raymond died at a time that was peculiarly unfortunate to his son—the termination of the first year of his college life. Already so much had been spent on Hugh's education, that but little had been laid by for the future. Certain casualties had prevented the rector from fulfilling his intention of insuring his life, so as to make a provision for his son and widow; and he died very suddenly, and in his prime, before he had been enabled to set apart from his income a sufficient sum to enable Hugh to complete his college career. In fact, it would have been abandoned, and Hugh would have sought some new sphere of life, had not Mr. Raymond's old college friend and neighbour, Sir Marmaduke Wrighton generously come forward and undertaken to supply all that was necessary for Hugh's maintenance while at college. He had already gained a scholarship, and Sir Marmaduke urged that it would be throwing away a livelihood, if he were not allowed to take his degree, and, possibly, be elected a fellow of his college, but, at any rate, be qualified to present himself as a candidate for orders, and for that clerical career for which he had professed a marked preference. By these arguments Mrs. Raymond permitted herself to be persuaded, and to accept Sir Marmaduke's liberality. And so Hugh continued at college until he had duly taken his degree; although, unluckily, he failed to obtain a fellowship.

CHAPTER III.

A DESPERATE ENGAGEMENT.

IN due course Hugh Raymond was ordained to a junior curacy in the large manufacturing town of Smokehampton. His stipend was but fifty pounds a-year, and lodgings were far from being cheap; there was therefore need of much pinching and contrivance to make the scanty income of the little family go far enough to provide them with a bare and decent maintenance. In the first instance, Margaret had wished to take the situation of a governess; but her aunt's sorrow at the prospect of losing her daily companionship was so real and poignant, that she abandoned her

design; and as she felt it to be impossible to remain
as an expensive burden upon her relatives, matters were
finally compromised by **Margaret** occupying certain
hours of the day in giving music and singing lessons,
—an employment for which her talents well fitted her.
So well did she succeed, **that,** within two months she
might have had more pupils than she had time at
their disposal; and she **received** more than one excellent offer for the situation of resident music-mistress
in boarding-schools; **but** her love for Mrs. Raymond
and the knowledge **that she had** become indispensable
to her, caused **her to decline all proposals that** would
have removed her residence **from those** dingy Smoke-
hampton lodgings where **her** cousin and aunt had fixed
their abode.

Did she ever tell them, I wonder, of that other
excellent offer made to **her by a brother of** one of her
pupils, and how she declined it—and *why* **she declined**
it? I think not. I fancy that she kept her own
counsel on this point, and had to tell **a** little bit of **a**
fib to her aunt in order to explain her reasons for so
suddenly refusing to give **the** young lady any more
music lessons. But though **she** did not go to that
dangerous house again, she continued elsewhere her
plodding daily round, and was not so tired of her
occupation but that she **also found both the time and**

the patience to train a **class of school** children into a very effective church **choir.** All **this time, she was** not only gaining her **own livelihood, but** was also contributing her share, and something beside it, to the expenses of lodging and housekeeping.

For the two years and a half that Hugh Raymond remained at Smokehampton, he **was** necessarily placed in the same relationship to his pretty **cousin** that he would have held had he **been her brother.** And, indeed, it was not until he had passed **some months** in the flats and swamps and **dulness of Cranston,** that the truth gradually **dawned upon him that he did** something more than miss Maggie's bright **looks, and** pleasant words, **and brilliant** playing and singing. **For his own** comfort **and** happiness, he would have been rejoiced if the household trio of Smokehampton could have been repeated at Cranston. But, in the first place, such a proceeding was scarcely practicable, on account of the impossibility of procuring suitable lodgings or renting any kind of tenement **between a** hundred-acre farm and a wattle-and-dab cottage : and, in the next place, Hugh felt that it would have been worse than a cruelty to have condemned his blooming cousin and his ailing mother to pass their days in the uncongenial atmosphere of Cranston parish and people. Acting, therefore, from **the** tenderest dictates of the heart, although sorely against his own natural desires, he persuaded his mother to consent to their separation, and to take a small house on the outskirts of Smokehampton, in which she and Margaret, with one servant to wait upon them, could live comfortably, and receive him for their guest whenever he was enabled to take a holiday from his Cranston duties. And, as this plan enabled Margaret to carry on her music lessons with her old pupils, it was unanimously adopted by the three persons concerned—with only three dissentient voices; but as these voices were but heart-whispers, they did not affect the decision.

Mrs. Raymond and her niece, therefore, went to live at Laurel Lodge (a laurel on a square yard of lawn before the sitting-room window had suggested to its proprietor the name for the house); and Hugh came to Cranston; and after no small difficulty—which did not, however, arise from any perplexity as to an embarrassment of riches in the choice of lodgings, but solely from the unwillingness of Mrs. Lupton to admit him as an inmate of her four-roomed cottage—settled down in two small low-ceilinged rooms, whose only merit was their cheapness. Here, with Mrs. Lupton to "do" for him, he was enabled to sit down at his leisure, and contrast his present life with the past.

Now came that awakening from his dream, of which the first change had come over him during his college days. From the total absence of any young ladies in Cranston and its immediate neighbourhood, and from the consequent avoidance of any disturbing elements to which their presence may have given rise, the Curate's introspections were absolutely forced upon the subject of his real feelings towards Margaret. As a matter of course, now that his eyes were opened by love, he very soon discovered that his cousin was something more to him than his sister (if she had lived) could possibly have been. He pondered over this discovery for some weeks, and looked at his newly-found treasure from every point of view; but, as he could not in any way regard it as the creation of Cranston *ennui*, or absence from Laurel Lodge, or the deprivation of all female society but that of Mrs. Lupton (a gaunt widow-woman who always wore her bonnet when she waited upon him at his meals) the Curate rationally came to the conclusion that he had that feeling towards his cousin which filled him with the desire to make her his wife.

After a few more weeks for further reflection, in order that he might not make any mistake on so momentous a subject, and after being daily more and more convinced that the new land of promise, of which he was

in sight, **was no** fog-bank or delusive oasis,—Hugh
wrote to Margaret, and told her of his discovery. She
replied very truthfully **and simply, th**ough without
being so very much surprised at the discovery,—reminded Hugh that she had not any property, and
delicately hinted that he had not much more ; and,
while she confessed that she returned her cousin's
affection, she expressed her opinion (with a sweet uncon-
sciousness of the wild inapplicability of her suggestion)
that it would probably be much better for his own
interests if he forgot her, except as a sister, and married one of the wealthy young ladies of whom, doubtless,
he would have such a choice in his new neighbourhood.

Hugh thought, with a shudder, of the half-dozen
hoydens who were the only people who could lay claim
to the title of " young ladies " in Cranston ; and he
began to write a very bitter and witty parody upon
" Locksley Hall, " in which he said,—

" As the wife is, **so** the husband, when he's mated **to a clown** ;
And the absence of her h's will have weight to drag his down ;

but, " the dark fen " and " level waste " and " rounding
gray " of Cranston were not so productive of poetry in
the Curate, as they might have been in Tennyson ; and,
after cudgelling **his** brains for an hour, and only producing a dozen lines of very poor parody, he desisted
from his attempts on the unwilling Minerva, and wrote

to his cousin in plain, and more congenial, prose.
Thenceforth, Hugh and Margaret were betrothed to
each other as firmly as though a solemn compact had
been mutually signed and sealed. There was very little
of what is commonly called "love-making;" for, the
article had been already manufactured by daily acts
and deeds intermeshed and woven into the web of
their lives; but, although their correspondence and
conversation was continued much as usual, in a matter-
of-fact, humdrum way, which might have appeared
excessively uninteresting and unloverlike to more
romantically disposed people, yet a new feeling had
undoubtedly invested their thoughts, words, and actions
with a complexion that they had not previously worn.
That problematical "some time or other" when their
path in life would be the same, was now the star that
guided them cheerfully onwards through the weary
round of their daily lot, and lent a lustre even to the
dulness of Cranston. With that star to cheer him,
the Curate would plod on through discouragement
with a better heart. Thoughts of Margaret were
mixed up with his parish work—in which she would be
such a help-meet; they cheered him in many a gloomy
hour; they bore him sweet company in many a long and
solitary walk; and they brightened his somewhat dreary
life in the swampy hollow of Cranston.

And this thought of Margaret and the future, did not exclude the companion thought of his widowed mother. She and Margaret went together in all his plans and day-dreams, and were joint mistresses of all his castles in the air. His mother, of course, would live with them : and, when (when !) he had saved sufficient to enable them to commence their married life, and to live with decent comfort, though with strict economy, he would procure a curacy in another parish, where they could again occupy one house, as at Smokehampton. He did not entertain the idea of introducing his ailing mother and blooming bride to rheumatic Cranston ; and he trusted that a curacy might elsewhere offer itself that should be equally as attractive in stipend, and much more so in situation and salubriousness. And so, with love's logic to aid him, he looked hopefully to the future, and endeavoured faithfully to discharge the important duties committed to his charge, and to labour for the best interests of his parishioners. The Cranston people had been sticking in the mud, both physically and morally, for so many years, that it could hardly be expected of them that they should emerge with cleanly minds and ways in a moment of time. In the modern Bœotia the revolution of manners and customs is not achieved in a day or hour ; and the bovine nature **of** the inhabitants of

Cranston required repeated applications of much sharper goads than the Curate thought fit to apply to them, ere they could be compelled to walk in fresh furrows.

A great objection to Cranston lay in its distance from Smokehampton, and, although the railways help poor lovers by their cheapness and annihilation of distance, yet the Curate, in his actual poverty, no less than from his desire to lay **by a store in** the Closeborough bank for that starry "**some time or** other,' thought himself compelled to **limit** his visits to Smokehampton to two in each year. **These were made at** Christmas and Midsummer, and were the more enjoyable because Margaret's holidays occurred at **those** seasons, and the cousins could thus dispose of the days as they thought best, and Margaret's only music lessons were bestowed upon Hugh, who had already made sufficient progress in the divine art to enable him to pick out Gregorians with one finger. But the Curate's holidays were but brief, and merely **lasted** from one Monday to the next Saturday week; for the sequestered position of Cranston cut him off **from** any Sunday help that might have been given him by neighbouring clergymen, and he was therefore compelled to procure a substitute at **an** expense of about three guineas for each Sunday. What with railway fare and

c

this Sunday substitute, Hugh's visits to Smokehampton were far too expensive treats to be indulged in
more than twice a-year; and so far as the practice of
austere self-denial went, the Curate of Cranston might
have been a monk of La Trappe.

However, he had Hope to live upon; and we know
from classical authority that credulous Hope cherishes
life, and ever tells us that there will be a better
morrow.

CHAPTER IV.

CHRISTMAS NIGHT.

HUGH RAYMOND had passed more than three years in
Cranston; and now, his fourth Christmas Day had
come, and was well nigh at an end. He was in his
little room, tired from his day's duties, and depressed
by a slight illness and by over-exertion. He had ex-
tinguished his lamp, and was sitting by the flickering
light of the fire, lost in meditation.

He was all alone in the house; for his landlady,
Mrs. Lupton, had asked him to spare her, in order that
she might pass the Christmas evening at her married
daughter's in the village. His thoughts, as usual,
had flown to Margaret and his mother, and he fervently

prayed that it might be the last Christmas Day that he might spend without them. He should not see them until four days had passed; for Sunday was very near, and he must stay for his duties on that day; but he had procured a substitute for the ensuing Sunday; so, in four days' time, he should be enabled to set out to Smokehampton for his brief Christmas holiday. But four days between him and happiness!

The house was very still: nothing was to be heard but the dull moaning of the wind, and the monotonous ticking of Mrs. Lupton's celebrated eight-day clock in the next room. Like its owner, it went about its work with an energy that was annoying from its very obtrusiveness, while, in face and figure, it was as tall, upright, grim, and clean, as Mrs. Lupton herself. Listening to the ticking of this clock, and the moaning of the wind, and shaping their combined sounds into a monotonous chant, the Curate closed his eyes, and fell into a sort of waking doze, in which, as though in actual sleep, he gave the reins to his fancies, and permitted them to bound over any obstacle. Chiefly did he contrast his present loneliness with that future scene that might be on the next Christmas night—his mother in a comfortable easy-chair on the one side, and, on the other, Margaret, with her chair drawn up close beside him, her left hand clasped in his, and, on the third finger, the wedding-ring. How well he could fancy her looking up into his face, with those deep, trustful eyes, in which he had never seen aught but love and truth, and then nestling still nearer to him, and saying,—" Dearest, how thankful I am that God has spared our mother to see us thus happy! How we thought and talked of you last Christmas night, with no one to speak to you, and cheer you, and tell you how much they loved you! and how we both prayed that, by another Christmas night, it might be *thus!* I can tell you this now!" And Hugh could picture to himself how she would nestle to him, as though nothing should ever part them more.

All this was very delightful to think of in a dreamy way, with closed eyes and lively brain; but it must be followed by the unclosing of the eyes, and the awakening from the day-dream. And Hugh roused himself from his reverie, and glanced round his lonely room, where the fire-light cast fantastic shadows into the cheerless corners, and felt the oppressive stillness of the house, with no sound save that monotonous ticking of the clock, and the dreary sobbing of the wind.

He was brooding over the wretched condition of a forlorn Robinson Crusoe of a bachelor Curate, cast on such a desolate island **as Cranston, in the** merry season of Christmas, when the **voices of** children, **outside** the cottage, reached his ears, and **their rustic carol** broke in upon **the oppressive silence.** They sang carols even in Cranston; **for carols** are old-fashioned things, and Cranston was an old-world place. There is always something affecting in the simple songs of children; and now, at this season, and at this hour, they seemed strangely pathetic. Something very like tears brimmed the Curate's eyes; but his **nerves were** unstrung by fatigue, and, as the night **was cold, a** profuse use of his pocket-handkerchief **was a circumstance** not to be wondered at. But, by the time that the carol was ended, he had relighted his **lamp, and had gone out to** meet the children, with **pleasant** friendly words. Then he made them **come into his** room, and have a warm at the fire, and sing him another carol, while he set out some plum-cake and cowslip-wine, that had been specially procured **for** the occasion. He bade them a happy Christmas, and God bless them: **and** they, emboldened by the unwonted feast, **laid aside** somewhat **of their** awkward, tongue-tied bashfulness, and also wished him a happy Christmas, and then went their way, and broke out into delirious shoutings.

He heard their noisy prattle die away in the distance, and then, with a shudder from the cold, turned into his solitary room, thankful that he had a warm fireside to sit by, and could pass the remainder of the evening in slippered ease. His landlady was to return by nine o'clock—an excessively dissipated hour for early village habits; but his watch pointed to ten before she made her appearance, full of apologies for being so late, but with the all-sufficient explanation that it was Christmas Day, "as only came but once'st a year"—a reason which, like Charity's cloak, is made to cover a multitude of shortcomings. Mrs. Lupton had also so much to tell of the joys of the evening, and entered into a narrative, so discursive and minute, of which Jacob and Rachel (her grandchildren) were the hero and heroine, that the Curate began to feel very drowsy, and to long earnestly for bed, even when the narrative had only reached to that early stage, in which the hero Jacob, as a reward for the singular aptitude **he had** shown in learning a verse of the Christmas Hymn, had been promised an orange, the very next time that his father went to Closeborough Market.

At length, Jacob **and** Rachel were disposed of, though not before their identity had been altogether lost in **the Curate's drowsy brain**; Mrs. Lupton wished him good night, and retired to bed; and,

after no long interval, the Curate followed her example, feeling thoroughly tired, and ready to sink to
sleep in an instant. But, **alas for the** vanity of human
wishes! he had **no** sooner tucked himself comfortably
under the clothes, than he heard the garden-gate
swing-to—then, a heavy step clumping up the pathway—then, a hearty rapping at the door. The Curate
sprang out of bed; a light from below glimmered
against his window-blind; and, opening the window,
he looked out, and asked,—

" Who's there ?"

" Oh, your Reverence ! " replied a **rough** voice,
which he recognized as belonging to a parishioner who
dwelt in the hamlet on the far side of the Common,
" I be main sorry to disturb you, I'm sure; but my
missus was took bad all of a sudden, afore we'd time even
to get Mrs. Jinks to her; and the long and the short
of it is—they're twins ! and they don't look as though
they'd be reared, and we shouldn't like **to have 'em**
put in the ground without so much as a prayer being
said over 'em; so I thought **as I**'d better come to you
at once'st, and be so **bold** as to ask **if you'd** be so good
as to come and name 'em ?"

" Certainly, Jones ! **wait for me** a moment, and I'll
come with you. There's nothing the matter, Mrs.
Lupton ! " he cried to his landlady, who had come to

her door, in some alarm at the unusual disturbance; "Mrs. Jones, of the Common, has been confined with twins——"

"Bless me, what a woman it is!" ejaculated Mrs. Lupton, as though the circumstance was some daring feat or act unbecoming a female.

"And I am going to baptize them. I shall lock the door after me, and shall probably not be away much longer than two hours. Good night! Jones is waiting for me below."

At the call of duty, the Curate had at once shaken off his fatigue, and, in a very short time, was accompanying Jones to the Common.

"I brought the lantern with me, your Reverence," said the man, "for it's quite unpossible to make out the way sitch a dark night as this, without a light. It was as much as I could do to keep it in; and I shouldn't have managed it, noways, if it hadn't been for lucifers. But I'm glad you've got a light of your own, sir, for it will make it all the better for you to see the way, which is the onkedest road as was ever put under a man's feet, and is quite a picking of the pockets of them as pays rates for keeping 'em in order."

"Yes, Jones, I think we might mend our ways in Cranston, in more senses than one; and the road, as you suggest, might be better." Here the Curate plunged into a rut, over his ancles in water, but emerged radiant and serene. "And, in the Fens and some other parts of England, there are roads that are worse, and far more dangerous, than these."

"Well, I should'nt ha' thought it were possible," said Jones; "I always looked upon we Cranston people as being the worst off o' anybody in that respect. But this sad land holds the wet till it's all of a soke and slabby, and welly fit for nought else but water-blobs and dodders."

Without their lanterns, the Curate and his companion could scarcely have made their way along the deep-set Cranston lanes; for the night was very dark, and the road was by no means so hard and direct that the traveller could feel the path with his feet, and tread carefully but securely. But, with the aid of the lanterns, they plodded on, through mud and mire, avoiding, as well as they were able, the deeper ruts and puddles that presented themselves as continually-recurring pitfalls before their feet; and so, up the winding lane, and out of the swampy hollow, and then forth upon the hill-top, and over the bare, bleak Common. The night was very cold, very dark, and very blustering. There were no stars, no moon, and no snow: it would probably have been much warmer if there had been snow. Out upon the open Common, there was a fierce, biting wind, that blew through them, making their eyes to water, and their teeth to chatter, and wringing their noses with sharp, unpleasant twinges. It was precisely the kind of night to excite within one's breast the desire to be a hare or rabbit, so as to be provided with a complete fur-suit; or, at any rate, to be a horse, and possess the privilege of wearing a nosebag in public. Mr. Jones, speaking the Anglo-Saxon of the district, pronounced the keen wind to be "a snitherer"; and, from its freezing coldness, would not have been surprised to find the end of his nose terminating in a "snipe," or icicle—pointed, indeed, like to the bill of that bird which has received its name from the length and sharpness of its beak.

The two strode on together, for the most part silently; for it was no night for a prolonged out-of-door conversation; and when Mr. Jones had remarked upon the roads and the weather, and had exhausted his formulary of apologies for dragging the Curate out on such a night, he had no more conversational power left. So they strode on in the cutting wind, over the bleak Common, tripping at the inequalities of the ground, slushing through the miry puddles, scaring the sheep (who were to be envied for their woollen blankets), and causing the mild-eyed oxen to look up with apathetic glances. Floundering and stumbling, they pressed across the waste, breasting the sharp breeze of the wintry night, and keeping their lanterns alight with as much difficulty as they could keep their feet.

At length a faint flickering ray of light was visible at some distance before them. "I hope," said the Curate, "that it's no Will-o'-the-wisp, or, as you Cranston people call it, a Jinny-buntail."

"No, your Reverence," replied Jones, much to the Curate's comfort, "yon's the hoosen; and I baint sorry to gain 'em. For what with stromping along in this snithen wind, and being knottled about my missus and the twins, I find myself quite in a guster." By which Mr. Jones meant that from combined excitement and exertion, he was somewhat out of breath. So was the Curate: and he was thankful when they got under the lee of the cottages, and out of the direct force of the wind.

CHAPTER V.

CHRISTOPHER AND CHRISTIANA.

THE faint light that had been their beacon during the last portion of their walk, denoted the house and the chamber in which the Curate's offices were required; and there was scarcely need for Jones to say "this way, sir," as he opened the door, and ushered Hugh Raymond into the cottage.

A few of the women neighbours were assembled in the lower room, busied about those little offices that were so much needed, and which the poor fulfil for each other with such amazing readiness. Passing through them, and up a step ladder, the Curate entered the crazy chamber where the hardest struggle in a woman's battle of life had so lately been fought. The roof sloped down on either side almost to the floor, and in many places, let in the moisture through the old thatch and broken plaister. There were three beds in the room—those for the children being even now filled with sleeping, or drowsy figures, huddled together for warmth, no less than from necessity; and on the middle of the floor, barely protected from the moisture dripping from the roof, was the bed whereon the mother was lying, with all the clothes that could be gathered together heaped over her. The room was bitterly cold, destitute of comforts, and even of many necessaries.

"It's but a poor ramshackle of a place, sir," said Mrs. Jinks, a neighbour who was in attendance. Indeed, she had been professionally engaged on the

occasion—a medical man being a too expensive luxury
—and was holding a lately-born child in her arms.
"And very awkard it is, as the chamber's not con-
venienced with a chimley. But we've done all we can
for her, poor dear! and made up a good fire down
below, so as to warm the house up, and hot her a few
broth and sich like."

"Am I in time?" asked the Curate, hearing no
infantile wailings, and seeing no movement in the
little bundle that Mrs. Jinks bore in her arms.

"Oh yes, sir, you're in time," she replied; "there's
no doubt about that; and it's very good of you, I'm
sure, to come so quick, specially in the middle o' the
night, and sich a night, and specially of it's being
Christmas night, which, took altogether, makes it the
kinder o' you to that poor dear and these poor dears.
I said at once'st," continued Mrs. Jinks, as the Curate
went up to the bed, and spoke quietly to its occupant,
"I said to Jones, who was all of a fidget and firk
about they babies being sich poor peakin things, bless
you, says I, when he soodled and dawdled, and was
afeared to go, bless you, I says, Mr. Raymond's that
deadly soft-hearted he'll come without any maundering,
and name 'em in a twinkling."

"But, do you think that the children will not live?"
asked the Curate, who, perhaps, called to mind what

the Prayer-book said about the " great cause and necessity" requisite for the ministration of private baptism of children in houses, and considered that Mrs.
Jinks' ideas on the subject might be somewhat hazy,
and that the present **case was** not one of necessity.

" Well, sir, you see," replied the nurse, "they babies **is so oncertain ;** sometimes the tiddiest 'll feed
out, and sometimes the likeliest is took off. That's
where it lies, sir; you're not safe with them a minit ;
and as long as they're gap-mouthed, they're that
whingelin, that they keep you all in the dithers."

The Curate did not exactly know what this meant,
but it sounded like something bad, and he therefore
concluded that his night's walk over the Common had
not been in vain. Still he was rather scrupulous, and
preferred to be on **the right** side of the rubric; so he
again put his question as to the probable life of the
twins.

" Well, sir," said Mrs. Jinks, " it is, as I may say,
what you was a preachin' on the last time I were at
Church—which were five sabbaths ago, but I can't
cudgle it to get there jist when I please, being strett
in other folks' affairs, and, sin' then, waitin' on young
Mrs. Perks with her first, her as lives by Muster
Ward's home-closen, and as you church'd last Sab-
bath," this was a parenthetical narrative, but Mrs.

Jinks continued her speech, as though it had not suffered from any interruption; "and, as you said, says you, we're here to-day, and gone to-morrow, says you. I remembers me the words well."

It was more than the Curate did. But, although he doubted the verbal accuracy of the quotation, he acknowledged the faithfulness of its spirit.

"And so, sir," said Mrs. Jinks, coming to the point, and gathering up the links in her chain of evidence, "there's no dependents to be put on they twins. This little mimmockin doan't look much like a nudgelin chump of a lad; and though t'other one niffled down its food like a good 'un jist at the first, yet it's but a poor stubby mite; and they're took that sudden wi' 'vulsions, that they might be quite quocken'd and black i' the face in almost no time. They doan't look as though they'd be reared; and though they're both alive at this present, yet, bless the Lord, it'd be a mercy if He'd take 'em to Hisself."

A moan from the mother, and a convulsive grasp of the tiny form that lay in her bosom, told that she would sooner part with life itself than lose that new source of heaven-sent affection, that now, in her time of great weakness, thrilled her with a greater joy.

"So I think it'd be but the right thing to name 'em, sir," said Mrs. Jinks, "though you're the best

judge o' that, of course, sir. But they look very peakin; and I'm sure it'd be the Lord's blessing if they
was took off, seeing as there are six mouths to fill already, and little enow' to put in their bellies—Jones
being slack o' work sin' harvest, and his fam'ly comin'
quick, and welly as many as a fezzle o' pigs."

Hugh Raymond went again to the mother's side,
and ascertained her wish that the twin children should
be baptized. They were a boy and girl, and it was
their father's desire that they should respectively be
named "Christopher" and "Christiana," in remem-
brance of the Christmas-day on which they were born.
Jones himself made this request in person, when he
had been summoned up the step-ladder by the Curate,
in order to be present at the ceremony. It was soon
performed; and when the mother, with her thin white
hand, again covered up the tiny form that lay upon
her bosom, tears checked the thanks she feebly strove
to utter. So Christopher and Christiana commenced
their lives; and, despite Mrs. Jinks' unfavourable prediction concerning them—a prediction chiefly based
upon the circumstance that the clock had been distinctly heard to strike thirteen instead of twelve on
the day of their birth,—despite this sure prognostic of
their quick decease, and despite the poverty and hard-
ships into which they had been flung, the twins lived,

and even thrived, long after the Curate had left them in that battered chamber of their birth.

"I'm main obleeged to you, I'm sure, sir," said honest Jones. "Clap another chump on, Mrs. Green, and set his Reverence a cheer agin the fire. Mebby, you wouldn't like to be lollupping all the night in sich a oncomfortable place as this'n; though you're right welcome to stay till the marnin's dahn, and longer."

"Oh, no!" the Curate said; he did not mind the darkness. He knew his way and had got his lantern; and, if he stayed till daylight, probably his landlady might be alarmed. "And I've got nothing to lose, Jones, except that," and he gave him a half-crown, "which I think you'd better keep for me, and turn it into something nourishing for your wife. So, if I should meet with such unlikely people as thieves, they can only take my lantern from me." And he forced the money upon poor Jones.

"There's summat as clats in my craw," said Jones, alluding to a hysterical feeling in his throat; "but I'm 'bleeged to you, though I han't got the speech to say so. You'll let me gwah wi' ye back whum, I hope, yer Reverence, and help to light you over the slabby road?"

The Curate would by no means permit such a thing: Jones had had walking enough already, and was much better at home where he could help to take care of his wife and children. The Curate also declined the invitation to " warm hisself agen the fire afore he flitted," on the ground that it would only make him the more susceptible of the cold on his way home; so, bidding them all good night and a happy Christmas, he went out alone into the midnight and thick darkness, with his lantern to guide him on his way.

CHAPTER VI.

THE CURATE MEETS WITH AN ADVENTURE.

THE weather had not improved during the half-hour that Hugh Raymond had been at the cottage. A cold sleet was now falling, and as, driven by the wind, it came pelting against his face, it hurt him like the stinging of bees. For some time he stumbled on amid the rushy bogs and puddles, until, confused and half-blinded by the drifting sleet, he found that he had wandered from the right track. There was no doubt about it; he had quite lost the path. He kept his face, however, steadily set in one direction; and so long as he did so, thought that he could not be very

far from wrong. So, stumbling and battling with the
sleet and wind, he made slow progress onwards.

Presently he found himself near to a clump of
trees; and, as he was well acquainted with the land-
marks of the country, he discovered the unwelcome
fact, that for the last half-hour he had been steadily
bearing away at right angles from Cranston. It was
certainly vexatious, for he was exceedingly tired, and
it was by no means a pleasant night to be abroad;
but he knew now where he was, and he could soon re-
gain his lost ground. So he bore manfully by the
skirts of a small spinny, and was just on the point of
striking off once more to the open Common, when the
light from his lantern flashed on something white
lying a few yards from him. He turned to look,—
stopped,—and looked again. A sudden fear possessed
him, and he shook with a cold tremor. What it was
had instantly flashed across his mind: but to reassure
and convince himself, he held out the lantern steadily, so that its light should stream full upon the white
figure.

Yes! it was not to be mistaken. His first dreadful
suspicion was confirmed; and through the driving
sleet, and by the aid of his flickering feeble light, he
knew that he was looking upon the prostrate form of
a woman bathed in blood. She lay at a short distance

from him, and somewhat below him, in a hollow of
the uneven ground, and near to the edge of the
spinny. She was clad in a long, white garment that
appeared to be her night-dress; one arm was tossed
over the head concealing the face, as though she had
been flung down in that posture; and from the
bosom streamed a great pool of blood, that had flowed
with a broad dabbled stain to her very feet. She lay
perfectly motionless, and had probably been dead for
some time.

The Curate felt paralysed at the dreadful sight, and
stood gazing at it through the drifting sleet, holding
out his lantern so as to throw its flickering light full
upon the body. He felt powerless either to speak or
stir. Only a few moments could have passed thus,
but they might have been hours from the intensity of
the emotions that were crowded into them. Then,
with a desperate effort, he moved towards the body.
As he did so, a great trembling seized upon him; a
fresh access of fear overpowered him, and the lantern
dropped from his hand. In a moment its light was
dashed out, and he was in total darkness. He clasped
his hands over his eyes, as though the terrible figure
might even make itself apparent to him through the
thick gloom. Then—his extreme terror inspiring him
with a certain sort of mad boldness, and fearing lest

his nervous system should utterly give way before the trial, if he paused another minute,—he dashed himself, as it were, against the body. Whether he fancied that life might yet be left within it, or whether he thought to lift it up, and bear it, if possible, to some human habitation, he could never determine; but acting solely on the impulse of a frenzied moment, without thought of what was to come, or what was to follow, he dashed towards the body, and clasped at the dress; and at the same moment, overcome by nervous agitation, heightened immeasurably by the fatigue that he had undergone, he fell insensible by the side of the body.

How long he lay he never knew. It may have been but for a few minutes; but, when he slowly returned to consciousness, the great fear that had possessed him had passed away, and his first confused thoughts were of the woman whose twins he had baptized. She had been in her night-dress; and, like a flash, that momentary thought had .linked itself to another. That murdered woman! horrible, most horrible! Now the memory of it dawned upon him. The biting sleet, and the bitter blast helped to revive him, and to awaken him to a full sense of his position. He was lying upon the ground, where he had fallen, and his hands were upon the murdered woman's dress.

Her dress? why, what was it? It shrank as he touched it; it was soft, and wet, and so thin and fragile that his hands passed through it. Strange! his senses were still but half awake! his brain was even now swimming from the effects of his fainting fit. Was it a spirit? he clutched at it desperately, but could not feel any substance.

A new terror began to seize upon him—a vague and unsubstantial dread which he could not have expressed, but which filled his whole frame. There, in the dead of that Christmas night, out in the darkness, on the bleak Common, the wind whistling around him, and the sharp sleet pelting over him, to be thus grappling with an unknown form and substance, was sufficient to have struck a terror into frames that were more coarsely knit, and into nerves that were less delicately strung, than were those of the Curate of Cranston. A sickening dread nearly choked him as he endeavoured to call for help; not that he thought that any help was nigh; but even the sound of his own voice might have cheated his imagination, and served to inspirit him with a false notion of companionship. As he did so, he again grasped at the figure, and, in a moment, felt what it was.

Paper.

Paper? yes! nothing more or less than a few yards

of tissue paper. His eyes were now becoming accustomed to the darkness, and he could distinguish the white paper pretty accurately. He began to gather it up, as well as its wet state would allow him to do so; and, at the one end, came upon some wires, and a piece of burnt sponge. The truth flashed across his mind. It was the body, not of a murdered woman, but of a collapsed fire-balloon, sent up, probably, at Closeborough, at some Christmas merry-making.

A sigh of relief escaped him; a load seemed to be taken from his mind; and, with the first revulsion of feeling at his discovery, he laughed long and heartily. Then he thought, what a dolt he must have been not to have seen this from the first, and to have perceived that the long stain of blood was nothing worse than a stripe of crimson tissue paper, a part of the ornament of the balloon. How every one would laugh at him when the story became known! even his own school children would jeer at his mistake.

And yet, how should they, or any one else, know of the circumstance, when there had been no witnesses to the scene? He would lock the secret in his own breast, or divulge it only to one who would not turn his adventures into ridicule.

So, this plan of action decided on, the Curate groped for his hat and stick and lantern; and then gathered up the cause of his fright, folded it as well as its soaked and tattered state would allow, and put it carefully into his pocket, as a proof both to himself and Margaret that he had not been dreaming, but had verily and truly seen that murdered woman, who had become a ghost, and had finally resolved herself, not into thin air, but into thin tissue paper.

The Curate was a long time in reaching his lodgings. He tumbled over ant-hills, and plunged through sedgy pools; and, after divers perils and muddy adventures, finally gained Mrs. Lupton's, where he let himself in very quietly, and slunk off to bed, and was soon in much too profound a slumber to dream either of murdered women or collapsed balloons.

CHAPTER VII.

SHORT AND TO THE PURPOSE.

Four days after, Monday morning had come, and the Curate was on his road to Closeborough, there to meet the train that should convey him to his mother and Margaret.

On his way, he had to pass through the village where the letters for Cranston were left, and from whence they had to be fetched by those who were anxious for such missives on any day between Saturdays. There were two letters for the Curate. One was from Margaret, who knew that he would call at the post-office on his way to the train, and had therefore written him a note to cheer him in his walk. You may be sure that he read this note at once; and that although every word was so hastily devoured, its contents agreed with him wonderfully well. Then he turned to the other letter. The hand-writing and crest seemed to be familiar to him: from whom could it be? as, clearly, to open it would answer the question, he broke the seal, and read as follows :—

" *My dear Sir,*

" *When I advised your present Rector to nominate you to the Curacy of Cranston—in which office I have reason to know that you have worked most laboriously, and, single-handed, have had to fight a very up-hill fight—I hoped that you would soon have something better worth accepting, and a sphere of duty more congenial to your tastes and feelings. From the force of circumstances, I have been unable hitherto to do what I wished to do from the first, and ask you to remove your residence from Cranston nearer to me. I am now*

D

enabled to do this, and to ask your acceptance of the Rectory of **Fairville,** which is now vacant, and of which I am the patron. I think you **must** know the parish, as it nearly adjoins the living held by my dear old friend, your late father. I need scarcely, therefore, describe it to you, or tell you that it lies in one of the healthiest and prettiest spots in the county; but I may as well say that its population (**which is purely** agricultural) numbered **327** at the last census: that the value of the living, with tithes and glebe, is not under £540: that there is a capital rectory-house, with four acres of land attached: that new schools have been erected, and that the church has recently been restored at my cost. I should be delighted to welcome as a near neighbour the son of a much-valued friend; and I sincerely hope that you will be able to meet my wishes on this point, and to do me the favour to accept my proposal. Your doing so will, I am sure, be a great boon to the somewhat-neglected parish of Fairville. With the best wishes of the season, believe me, dear sir,

" *Very truly* **yours,**

"MARMADUKE WRIGHTON."

" *Wrighton Court, December* **26.**"

How the **Curate** of Cranston got to Closeborough, he knows **as little** as how he **got to** his lodgings on that memorable Christmas night: but he *did* get to the station, and in time for the train.

But whether or no he accepted Sir Marmaduke's offer, and whether or not he married Margaret in the next merry month of June, and had his mother to live with them at the pretty rectory, I must leave you to guess. But this one thing I *may* tell you; that, when Christmas night again came round, Hugh Raymond was at Fairville Rectory, and there told to his mother and Margaret (who, by the way, wore a wedding-ring) the little tale that I have now told to you.

A SMALL WATER-PARTY.*

Perhaps you don't know Norman Grange?—and if
    so, you've a loss, I assure you.
'Tis the prettiest spot you could find in the beautiful
    county of Blankshire,
And of all county families there, the palm is borne off
    by the Mortons.

Comes the Paterfamilias first: tall, smiling, complacent,
    and portly;
With his face finely colour'd with health, and per-
    chance by some magnums of claret;
With his coat of the bluest of blue, and its buttons
    the brightest of brass;
And the whole of his costume, as far as his wife and
    the fashion allow him,
Partaking of that remote cut, assign'd by unanimous
    counsel

---

* In rhythmical hexameters, *i. e.* English words whose long and
short quantities are to be scanned by the ear, and not by the rules
that govern Latin dactyls and spondees.

To old English Gentlemen, when there were pigtails,
  and powder, and Tories.

Well rides he up to the hounds, on one of his thorough-
  bred hunters,—

A study for Landseer or Grant, as he sits there compact on the pig-skin,—

A model for Leech, who would masterly sketch him
  as nobody else could,—

Manfully facing a bullfinch, and flying o'er raspers
  and five-bars,

While the woods echo back his rich voice as he cheerily
  yoicks his harkforrud !

A dead shot is he with the birds, and the terror of
  partridge and pheasant,

Keeping up all the sports of the field, as an old English gentleman should do.

A Solon he is on the Bench—at all the Board-meetings
  a Draco ;

Terrible, too, on the Rates, and at Quarter Sessions,
  tremendous !

As Commissioner, too, of the roads, an authority
  great as Mac Adam ;

As a Magistrate, upright and stern ; as a Guardian,
  fierce as a lion ;—

But in all the relations of life, affable, frank, and
  good-hearted.

When he rides forth o'er his fields, or walks at foot-
    pace through the village,
The white-headed children rush forth, and pull at their
    hair for a greeting;
And the hearts of the Clodpoles are glad, when the
    Squire pulls up to address them.
Great is he then on the crops; learned on subsoil, and
    compost;
Knowing on Mechi and Pusey; and quotes Mr. Hux-
    table's porkers;
Draining, and short-horns, and lime, and oil-cake, and
    Leicesters, and fallows,
And words to which Cockneys can't give any due
    agricultural notion,
(Although they once got up the "Georgics" by rote
    when they went to Grey Friars,)
Fly about like a juggler's brass balls, whenever he
    talks with his tenants,
Who respect "Squoire Morton as much—why, as dang
    it! the Queen or Prince Holbut!"

Comes his good-natured better-half next, rustling in
    richest of satin;
With that well-preserved comeliness that's so peculiar
    to matrons of England,
Where the roses of beauty and health can bloom with-
    out rouge and cosmetics.

What she was in her maidenly prime, we may judge
    from her fair eldest daughter,
Miss Lizzie, of " sweet seventeen," who came out to
    the world this last season,
And in her young rosebuds reflects the expanded full
    bloom of her mother.
Such a friend to " the young folks," ne'er lived as
    good Mrs. Morton of Blankshire !
To chaperone motherless girls—to giving of parties, and
    picnics,
And filling her house full of guests—no woman there
    ever lived like her !

Not long since she sent me a note, with a pressing and
    kind invitation,
That I'd come the next week to the Grange where a
    party would then be assembled ;
" But come on the Thursday, be sure ! for then, we've
    a small Water-party ;
We shall have a lunch-dinner at three, and afterwards
    go on the river."

I accepted (of course !) ; and next week, having sent
    on my bag and my baggage,
I over to Norman Grange rode, and reach'd there in
    time for the luncheon.

As I took the short cut through the park, it brought
    me out just by the stables.

And there, in the courtyard, I found a sample of each
    kind of carriage,

From the stately old family-coach to the stylish, but
    fast-looking, dog-cart;

Betok'ning our party that day was one of the largest
    dimensions.

And so I soon found that it was—a regular county
    assembly,

Among whom, as the newspapers say, "we noticed the
    Earl of Trinorben;"

Her Ladyship too, with her sons, the little Lord Gules,
    and his brother;

With the Broughtons, the Dalrymples, Hayes; the
    Gurdons, Saint Quintins, and Wyatts;

The Darnells, and Campbells, and Thorneys; the
    Haslewoods, Howards, and Clintons;

And all the best families round, and all the presentable
    Curates.

The children had also been ask'd—and all who had
    juveniles brought them;

And since many could boast that their quivers were
    pretty well furnish'd with arrows,

The infantile prattle and laugh were decidedly in the
    ascendant.

We all, until feeding-time came, wander'd about in the
    gardens;
And a beautiful prospect it was to see all the beautiful
    women
In their many-hued muslins and silks, go gleaming
    about 'mid the flow'rs,
The loveliest bouquets of all, and where all was fair, yet
    the fairest,
Promenading the terrace in groups, while their children
    play'd gaily around them;
Strolling about through the park, and flashing, like
    wandering sunbeams,
Down the broad avenue where the elms threw their
    quivering shadows.

In a spacious marquee in the park, close by the Italian
    garden,
There was the luncheon laid out—comprising, of course,
    every dainty
That French cooks had ever devised, or confectioners
    ever invented,
A *déjeûner* ample and varied—and not like to some I
    could mention
That are more ornamental than useful, and made up of
    garnish and flowers—

But a good and substantial repast, to which a great
 gong boom'd the summons.

I was delightfully placed! On one side I'd Miss
 Lizzie Morton;
On the other, the fair Mrs. Hayes, with her two olive-
 branches beside her—
Their little cheeks rosy and soft as the peaches they
 then were devouring.
She was one of those capital people that shine with
 full force when they're married;
And few can enchant us so much as a nice little well-
 married woman,
Who has passed Hymen's rubicon long, and the
 honeymoon's billing and cooing,
And has settled down into the stern and practical
 duties of marriage,
With little, live, miniature shapes of her husband and
 self to hang round her,
And invest her with motherly cares, and the dignity
 too of a matron.
How delightful is she to converse with! so unreserved,
 easy, and piquant;
With that free confidential discourse denied to the
 maidens of England,

Whom the laws of "society" bind in conventional
    stays, and strait-waistcoats,
And, denying them freedom of speech, thus cripple
    their natural feelings,

Quite as much as in China their feet would be pinch'd,
    and distorted, by Fashion;
So that Miss on my right, may not say what Mamma,
    on my left, says so freely;
For Etiquette then would step in and say, " You are
    sinning against me,
Thus to talk with that gentleman, whom you treat as
    a man and a brother !
Pray remember that others might think your affections
    were his, for the asking !"
So, to quite put an end to these gross and very improper
    suspicions,
Poor Miss puckers up her sweet lips, and, to use a
    most vulgar expression,
Picks and looks at her words, e'er she speaks, and
    sinks into common-place parlance.
Thus it is that the gushings of youth are frozen and
    chill'd in their fountains,
And often, it may be, choked up by "society's"
    heartless conventions.

But whilst Mrs. Hayes and her talk are thus my attention engrossing,

The luncheon has greatly progress'd, and the champagne as greatly diminish'd;

And young ladies—who probably made a very good
luncheon ere starting—

Lean back in their seats, and declare, "Not a drop
more! now really I couldn't!"

But the children, who cannot as yet entertain such
ethereal notions,

Whilst they see all those beautiful sweets, and the
tempting pine-apples untasted,

Would never give over, unless their mothers cried,
"Hold, enough!" for them.

At length—away sail the ladies and children, the
gentlemen leaving behind them

Disconsolate, as, of course, men always are when the
ladies have left them:

But trying to drown their regrets, when the Squire puts
in this suggestion,

" We've just a few minutes to spare before we go down
to the river:

You'll find this most capital port, but there's claret
for those who prefer it.'

Then, when one or two **hobbledehoys,** who are secretly
    shaving for whiskers,
Look vacant, and wild in the eyes, and in language
    are foggy and misty,
Some one winks to the Squire, and says, " We'd better,
    p'r'aps, go to the ladies."

The Swinney, as every one knows, is the principal river
    of Blankshire,
And flows with a beautiful sweep, by the Norman-
    grange mansion and meadows.
The boat-house thrusts out its black nose from under
    a fringe of green willows,
And thither we all of us troop, and are marshall'd
    with skill to our places.

When a young man at Oxford, the Squire was great in
    all matters aquatic,
And, as captain, had got up his boat by degrees to the
    head of the river ;
So that when he left College he brought the St. Vitus's
    boat to the country.
And there, with the four oars, it was drawn up to the
    steps at the landing—
An eight-oar cut down to a six, with the stern fitted
    up for the ladies ;

No cranky and modern outrigger, but a good patent-
    safety flat-bottom.

The rowers are chosen, and strip; and the boats, one
    by one, are in motion;
Then, a snugly-caparison'd barge receives all the rest,
    and the children.

The Squire to me has been kind; of St. Vitus's boat
    I'm the coxswain;
And the gay tassell'd cords of the rudder I tug with
    a nervous excitement,
For the ten chosen belles of the party depend upon
    me for their safety.
The Squire pulls stroke, as he did in the days of his
    youth and his vigour;
And the rest, though they keep not their time, nor
    feather "with skill and dexterity,"
Yet are passable oars on the whole, and decidedly
    jolly young watermen.
Charley Grey, of the Guards, who performs pretty well
    on the cornet-à-piston,
Has "come with his music," and lies in the bow, lest
    the ears of the ladies
Should be pierced with the sharp, ringing notes, which
    the distance will mellow to sweetness.

The St. Vitus's boat takes the lead; and we sweep
    with a spurt, up the river,
And our pennon streams out in the breeze, as Grey
    blows a blast of defiance;
While I, who am single, and flirting with ten flirting,
    single young ladies,
Have lost all my presence of mind in a pleasing
    delirium tremens,
And steer the St. Vitus's boat slap into a bed of tall
    rushes!
The blast of defiance is hush'd, and mild objurgations
    succeed it,
And the oars are all rapidly shipp'd, while the ten
    bonnets duck to the rushes;
And I with the reeds and confusion am cover'd as
    though with a garment.

We drift out at length; and, of course, I promise
    amendment of steering;
And we soon leave the shouts of derision the four-oars
    and barge have sent to us;
Then, in a soft, green, floating shade, underneath the
    cool droop of the willows,
We lay-to awhile, and look out for the rest from our
    watery arbour;

And the ladies bend over the side, and pluck at the
    white water-lilies,
Or the more sentimental forget-me-nots, fringing the
    banks of the river
With their flowery masses, that seem as though bathed
    in the bright blue of heaven.
'Tis pleasant to look up the stream, as the four-oars
    come dropping down to us,
While the heavier barge lags behind, with its freight
    of mammas and their cherubs.
The breeze bears their musical laughter, the water re-
    flects their fair figures ;
The oars cleave the stream into ripples that break up
    the many-hued shadows ;
The silvery willows are fringed with a brightness that
    seems like a halo ;
The pastures are dappled with kine, cud-chewing,
    lazily lying ;
The haymakers, ruddy and brown, are at work in the
    sweet-smelling meadows ;
The bean-fields throw out their perfume, and the reeds
    pipe their Pandæan music ;
And the sun, sinking low in the west, lights up all
    with his own golden splendour.

It is pleasant to see this, and float through the cool of
    the evening shadows
With ten pretty girls by your side, and you wishing
    you'd ten hearts to give them.
And p'rhaps it is better for me that the people who
    manage the office
Where I'm just now insuring my life, were not pre-
    sent to see, and report me.
Disease of the heart, or at least some affection in that
    tender quarter,
Would have surely been laid to my charge, and my
    bachelor's life proved in danger,
And the risk I was running, of course, would have
    raised the expense of insuring.
However, I craftily cover'd my love-germs with heaps
    of loose small-talk,
And Spartan-like, never cried out while my heart was
    thus being devour'd.

The star of the evening comes out ere we have come
    off from the water,
And the twilight is gathering round as we turn us
    away from the river.
While Grey of the Guards trumpets out the air that
    is called "Isle of Beauty."

Then—when the coffee's been served, the tuning of
　harps and of fiddles
Gives the prelude to other delights, and summons us
　all to the ball-room ;
And there, demi-toilet asserts its *negligée* charms over
　full-dress.
Quadrilles unto waltzes succeed, and polkas are polked
　to distraction ;
And " Pop Goes the Weazel" is tried, but condemn'd
　to be thence shelved for ever ;
And " La Tempête " is danced in its stead, and seems
　to give great satisfaction ;
And the juveniles vanish with speed, and leave the
　room free for their elders.

The ball-room's three windows lead out to the ter-
　raced Italian garden,
And there by the moonlight we stroll, to cool from the
　heat of the dances.
And some loving couples are seen extending their
　walk and their converse,
Down the broad avenue where the elms make a cheque-
　work of shadows.
Dangerous strolling, indeed !—the first figure of Pop
　Goes the Question.

But ethereal joys must succumb to material needs and
    necessities;

And, while **Lubin** is piping his love, his thoughts may
    be busy with—supper!

And great is the charm of the supper, besides the
    mere business of eating:

That we will leave to the gourmand! Give *us* the
    light feasting of reason,

And the flow of the soul that will spring like the
    champagne's own brilliant bubbles,

And burst into sparkles of wit, whose grave is the
    pleasures they rose from!

Dancing commences again; and the hobbledehoys,
    growing bolder,

No longer as wallflowers stand, nor sheepishly lurk up
    in doorways,

But, primed with champagne, rush to polkas, and
    madly e'en think of a *deux-temps*,

And flounder about on the toes of the good-natured
    girls who will take them.

Lady-mothers at length get to gape, and, unlike the
    song's " winking May-buds,

'Gin to " close, not to "ope sleepy eyes," and look
    most unnaturally drowsy ;

And, though their fair daughters protest they must
    throw overboard many partners,

Yet all's to no use! and the prayer, "but just one
    more dance," won't be heard more ;

And, "you know your papa never likes for the horses
    so long to be waiting."

So the hens take their chickens away ; and wraps are
    in great requisition ;

And the steps and the doors of the carriages bang
    with a loud demonstration ;

And the rattle of wheels on the gravel dies faintly
    away in the distance ;

And the last " Sturm Marsche Galop" is whirl'd, and
    the last "good night " wish'd to the hostess ;

And the last ringing laughter of girlhood floats lightly
    its heavenly music ;

Till 'tis drown'd by the cornet-à-piston on which
    Charley Grey is expressing

That till morning we do not go home, to end this
    our Small Water-party !

"VICTORIA REGIA."

[NOTE.] The *Victoria Regia* (as it was afterwards called) the magnificent queen of the water lilies, was discovered, in 1837, by Sir Robert Schomburgh, in a hitherto unvisited river in British Guiana. Drawings of its gigantic dimensions were exhibited in England; but, as the seeds which had been brought over did not germinate, the drawings were generally thought to be the artistic fictions of an imaginative traveller. Fresh seeds, however, were sent over by Dr. Rodie, of Demerara, and by Mr. J. Carter (in 1847), which were more successful, and germinated both at Kew and at Chatsworth. The latter flowered first (on Nov. 9th, 1849), and a leaf and flower of the plant were presented by Mr. Paxton to Her Majesty and Prince Albert. The house built for the reception of the Victoria Regia was planned from designs furnished by the plant itself! These are Mr. Paxton's own words :—" Nature was the engineer in this case. You will perceive that nature has provided it with longitudinal and transverse girders and supporters, on the same principle that I, borrowing from it, have adopted in this Building." Seven months after this, when the Great Exhibition Building Committee had rejected the designs of the 273 competitors, in favour of a plan of their own, which was so unsightly, cumbrous, and expensive, that it was at once condemned by the unanimous voice of public opinion, at this crisis stepped in Mr. Amateur-Architect Paxton, and cut the Gordian knot in the most satisfactory manner. His design for a Crystal Palace of iron and glass, on the same principle as the *Victoria Regia* house at Chatsworth, was first published to the world in the pages of the Illustrated London News for July 6th, 1850. What followed upon the publication of this design is now a matter of history ; and the connection that thus arose between a Water-Lily of British Guiana and the Crystal Wonder of the Nineteenth Century is also a matter of history.

'Neath the burning sun of a torrid clime
    All day I bathed in the waters cool ;
And my snowy breast, at the touch of Time,
    Blushed rosy red* to the amorous pool.
A child of nature I lived, and loved
    Thus on the waters to float all day :
To lazily lie by the waves upmoved,
    And to sport with the billows in idle play.
There, with a bevy of sisters, I grew
    In grace, and in beauty, and still as a dream—
Wilderness water-nymphs, hidden from view,
    And longing to die on our well-loved stream.
We sighed not for wealth—we had emerald trees,
    The jewelled birds and the sapphire sky ;
And our forest bath, 'neath the rippling breeze,
    Into sparkling diamond sprays would fly.

Ah ! well I remember the fatal time,
    When a new sound startled us all to fear ;
When the plash of oars with their murmured chime,
    Smote on the listening Solitude's ear.

* The white blossom of the Victoria Regia gradually assumes a pink tinge on the upper part of the petal.

Breathless we stood for we could not flee ;
　　Was it fear that rooted us to that spot ?
The sailors shouted aloud for glee,
　　As their boat to our unknown wilderness shot ;
They dashed among us with open arms,
　　And each one eagerly seized his prize ;
And our breasts throbbed quickly with soft alarms,
　　As we met the glance of their longing eyes.
I, by the lord of the sailors was claimed,
　　And he lifted me tenderly into the boat ;
And while the red sunset in anger flamed,
　　Our loved birds watched us away from them float.

A thousand miles he bore me away,
　　To his cold, cold land in the northern clime,
And I pined and drooped from day to day,
　　As I thought on the joys of the olden time.
Yet it seemed ungrateful thus to moan
　　O'er the golden hours all past and gone ;
Though lost was the sun of the torrid zone,
　　The light of affection upon me shone.
My captor loved me, and gave me wealth,
　　And built for my pleasure a fairy-like home,
Where, screened from cold, in sunshiny stealth,
　　I joyfully bathed 'neath a crystal dome.

Then the colour came to my cheeks again :
    And I sought to repay his loving care :
And my new home saw me as gladsome as when
    My lips were kissed by a southern air.

Then I went to a prouder palace by far—
    A palace vast, with a hundred bowers,
Where the diamond gleamed like a wintry star,
    And coloured gems mocked the gem-like flowers.
All around were hangings of Tyrian dyes,
    And plashing fountains leapt and gushed ;
And cunning statues charmed the eyes,
    Though their life was in marble silence hushed ;
Palms spread their feathery fans on high,
    But they failed to touch the rainbow'd dome ;
And pulses of music throbbed audibly
    Through the mazy courts of my palace home.
With the flowers and fountains, and fanlike palms,
    Sweet recollections would round me throng,
For the buried thoughts that mem'ry embalms,
    Will rise at the last, though forgotten long.

FOREIGN AIRS AND NATIVE GRACES.

In the second series of the " Recreations of a Country Parson " we read the following :—" I remember how, a year or two since, that contemptible ' Ratcatcher's Daughter,' without a thing to recommend it, with no music, no wit, no sentiment, nothing but vulgar brutality, might be heard in every separate town of England and Scotland, sung about the streets by every ragged urchin, while the other songs of the vivacious Cowell fell dead from his lips " (p. 68).

Now, although we never heard "the vivacious Cowell" sing the song in question, yet we *have* heard it (from a middy's lips) many years before the " vivacious " Cowell had disentombed it from the grave of the past, and started it on its new career of popularity. Like " Villikins and his Dinah," "The Ratcatcher's Daughter" was merely an old ballad revived ; and, as we write this, we have before us an edition of the ballad,

E

bearing date 1842, and illustrated with seven clever
lithographic drawings by Miss Brigstocke.   But why
we now more particularly draw attention to the above
extract from the Scotch minister's " Recreations " is, to
notice his remark, that the song has " no music," notwithstanding that its melody was sung by all the ragged
urchins in England and Scotland—a fact which, we
think, would alone have been a sufficient proof that
the ballad *had* some real "music" in its composition.

But what is the fact ? Perhaps if we were to assert
that the air of " The Ratcatcher's Daughter" was by
Mozart, we should appear to be stating an improbability,
if not an impossibility.   And, if we were to tell our
Country Parson that, in the Kirks of his native land, and
in many of the churches and chapels in England, he
may have heard a hymn sung to the melody of "The
Ratcatcher's Daughter," we dare say that he would
receive our statement with polite incredulity.   And yet
both our statements, if not absolutely correct to the very
letter—that is, to each individual musical note—yet
are, in the main, quite true.   For, the Psalm tune (common in certain congregations) which goes by the name
of "Belmont," is an adaptation of an air by Mozart ;
and if " Belmont " be rather briskly sung, it will be
found that one is singing the melody of "The Ratcatcher's Daughter"—and a very pretty melody it is,

notwithstanding that the Country Parson says there is "no music" in it. Since he can write essays that are "Sermons in polka-time," let him try to sing the hymnal "Belmont" in "Ratcatcher's Daughter" time, and he will find that he is singing a melody by Mozart, which certainly has "music" "to recommend it." One trial will prove the fact—as the advertising grocers say: and the singers of "Belmont" can lay to heart that saying of Wesley's that " the devil must not have all the good tunes." A sermon in polka-time would sound very differently from the same sermon preached with slow solemnity; just as the same notes, when played *allegro* and *penseroso*, would convey very opposite impressions.

Thus, we have known an instance, where a certain secular air played in a church very slowly, and in chords, threw the musical rector, not into displeasure, but into ecstacies with the impressive beauty of its solemn melody. Of course the rector was not in the secret; and the next day, he asked his friend, the amateur organist, for a copy of his organ-piece. " Before I give you the copy," was the reply, " would you not like to hear me play it on this piano-forte?" " Oh, yes!" " Then, for a change, I will play in a rather quicker time." And he *did* play it; and the tune he played was Rodwell's " Nix my dolly pals fake away!" out of "Jack Sheppard." And the feelings

E 2

of that musical Country Parson may be more easily
imagined than described.

Perhaps many modern popular airs, and "nigger
melodies," might be traced to high originals. Thus,
the tune of "Buffalo Gals" is said to be taken from an
old air by Glück; and that of "Old Joe" from an air in
Rossini's "Coradino." There is an adagio piece of
music existing in MS. at Oxford, and stated to be the
piece of music performed at Fotheringay, during the
execution of Mary Queen of Scots. It is similar in
character to the Dead March in "Saul," and has an
equally solemn and pathetic effect when played in slow
time; but when played in fast time it resolves itself
into the old English lively tune of "Jumping Joan."

THE SPRING OF LIFE.

" I am content to die—but, oh ! not now !"
            The Child of Earth.—(By the Hon. Mrs. Norton.)

Oh, 'tis hard to die when the spring has come,
In her grass-green robe, to her sunny home;
When the Winter King has resign'd his sway,
And his icy palace has melted away;
When the spring is come and the summer is nigh,
'Tis hard, dear mother, indeed, to die !

When the flowers are springing from out of the earth,
To deck the mother that gave them birth;
When the opening blossoms of orchard-trees
Are scattering sweets to the passing breeze;
When all is bright as the blue, blue sky,
'Tis hard, dear mother, indeed, to die !

When the rose is unveiling her blushing breast
To her nightingale lover in wild unrest;

When the butterfly floats so blithely along,
And the wild bee hummeth his drowsy song;
When we hear in the folds the young lambs cry,
'Tis hard, dear mother, indeed, to die!

When the beautiful birds, in their wild-wood home,
Sing 'neath their palace's leafy dome;
When the wooded heights and the valleys ring
With the echoes of their sweet carolling;
When the hidden cuckoo is heard hard by,
'Tis hard, dear mother, indeed, to die!

When the brook comes babbling through the dell,
Telling soft tales to the wild bluebell;
When the hyacinth blooms, and o'er each hedgerow
The May-buds scatter their blossoms of snow;
When the winds breathe soft as love's first sigh,
'Tis hard, dear mother, indeed, to die!

I would wish, on my death-bed, to lie, and see
The green leaves robing each forest-tree;
I would wish to look, in my latest hours,
On the brightest hues of the fairest flowers;
And to watch the sun sink in the golden sky;
Yet, 'tis hard, dear mother, in spring, to die!

I would not die when the wintry snow
Clothes with a death-shroud the earth below,
Hiding from mortal eyes and sight
All that is beautiful, fair, and bright;
When trees rear their skeleton forms on high—
I would not, dear mother, in winter, die.

But, I would die when the autumn's gold
Should warm the damps of the churchyard mould ;
To wake from my wintry tomb, to rise
To the spring eternal beyond the skies ;
But, oh ! just now, when the summer is nigh,
'Tis hard, dear mother, indeed, to die !

TO —— ON HER BIRTHDAY.

JULY 23.

Not in the cheerless winter of the year,
When sickly suns glare dimly o'er the snow,
When trees are stripp'd of yellow leaf and sere,
And rivers rage, and rough winds rudely blow,—
But in the sweet time of the Summer's sun,
When all is bright, and balmy breezes blow,
The journey of thy lifetime was begun.
The merry sunshine warm'd thee with its glow;
The rosy Summer kiss'd thee into life,
And ran the hot blood dancing through thy veins;
The zephyrs lull'd thee with their softest strains,
And Love, thy pathway strew'd with fairest flowers.
Dear child of Summer! whether maid or wife,
May your life's dial show but sunny hours.

THE LITERARY ABUSE OF ADJECTIVES.

One of the commonest vices in literary composition is the abuse of the Adjective. When properly treated, the adjective is one of the most useful parts of speech; but when put to more than its due work, it becomes weak and good for nothing. The chief sinners in this vice are fair sinners: the poor adjectives are abused and ridden to death far oftener by lady-authors than by males.

It has been said, that when a woman has the driving or riding-reins in her hands, she never ceases from fidgeting at her horse with the whip; and it is the same with these literary hacks of adjectives— when a woman has a pen in her hand, she is always "touching up" her composition with them, not being content with giving one where it is required, but dis- tributing them by twos and threes with a great flourish and lack of discrimination. They are, to her narra-

E 3

tive, what the fidgeting touches of the whip would be to her horse,—he gets on none the quicker for them, and they do not improve his disposition; and though her flourish of the whip, or pen, may be given with a grand air, yet, after all, it means nothing, and might be much better omitted, so that the sharp, well-placed lash, or adjective, might fall with full force in the proper quarter.

For there is nothing more forcible in literary composition than this often-abused adjective, if it be skilfully chosen and applied after due thought. But Mediocrity cannot afford to think, or to blot its manuscript. Its *copia fandi* is after that kind of watered eloquence that abounds in the small-talk of ladies; and adjectives pour forth in an unhesitating and indiscriminating stream. This is unpremeditated art certainly; but the value of the performance is terribly diminished by its superficial character. Volatile spirit there may be; but little body or depth. The composition is attained by clearing the steps of thought at a bound; but little meditation precedes the act, and no revision follows it. If it did, how many of those abused and weakening adjectives would be struck out! But Mediocrity either cannot see this, or cannot afford to do it, and takes their crowded presence as a sign of strength and wealth. But is it so ? It is very true that the adjective, when well thought out and skilfully applied, can, with a happy touch, change the bare outline of the substantive into a picture full of light and sensuous colour; and that it will give meaning to what was obscure, and lend a value to that which was worthlesss.

Macaulay and Tennyson are two note-worthy modern instances of the consummately skilful use to which the adjective may be put in literary composition. With them its use is a matter for due thought and careful selection, and it is not abused by being pitchforked into a sentence, merely that it may swell that sentence or eke out the rhythm. With them, the adjectives do not come trooping in crowds, jostling and elbowing each other in a confused medley, but are assigned to their proper and individual stations. As a rule, and except in certain instances where there is a special end in view, and in such tricky poems as Southey's *Lodore,* the increase in the number of adjectives does but diminish their power. However bright and attractive they may be in themselves, yet they are but as the poppies amid the corn.

An indiscriminate use of their wealth is like indiscriminate charity, which, though it may now and then be happily applied, yet on the whole does more harm than good. The riches must be judiciously

distributed in the proper quarters ere their real
benefit can be appreciated. However strong an
author may be, yet his strength is changed to weakness, when it is expended on a thoughtless use (or
rather, abuse) of adjectives. A plethora of adjectives
is anything but a sign of literary health; and the
hampering of plain words with a string of gaudy
ornaments is far from being an evidence of pure taste.
The very prodigality of invention occasionally leads a
young writer to fling away his adjectives with a reck-
less profusion that sometimes borders upon the ridiculous, and at all times gives his readers a task, that
may prove wearisome, to possess themselves of the
glittering gems.

This was strikingly the case with Alexander
Smith, in his "Life-drama." In his love for "word-
painting," he terribly abused unoffending adjectives,
and, as the Yankees say, piled them up too "moun-
taynious:" and, it is in word-painting, however
brilliant, that we too often meet with the abuse of
adjectives from those who have a fatal facility for their
fatal felicity. But this is never the case with the
great masters of the English language, whose simplicity of style is a safeguard against their committing
the offence in question. But, while the literary abuse
of the adjective by the hands of Talent is a subject for

regret, what can we say to the intolerable treatment that it has to endure from Mediocrity? There is some excuse for extempore preachers and speakers; for, while they are heaping up adjectives (which are generally synonymous) they are gaining time for fresh thought—though often, in their cases, the adjectives are only used as decent coverings for their nakedness of thought, and their literary value sinks to the level of the vain repetitions of a Stiggins, or Chadband.

But there is no excuse for those who have the time allowed them to write down their thoughts, and to correct them when written. They are culprits (and, generally, feminine culprits) beyond the hope of pardon, who can deliberately send forth into the literary world such poor abused adjectives as that represented by the word "sweet"—which are presumed to give an indefinite saccharine flavour to the composition,—but which, in truth, do but tend to class it in that barley-sugar-and-lollipop species of literature, wherein we find such a terrible abuse of the Adjectives.

THE KINGFISHER.

A SUDDEN flash of bluest light,
 The Kingfisher flew o'er the pool :
I track'd it in its glitt'ring flight,
 Where willows made a shadow cool.
The burning sun was in the sky,
 But no ray pierced that shelter'd spot ;
Yet, like a flash, the bird flew by,
 Bluer than blue forget-me-not.

And thus, I thought, in Life we see,
 In every dim and darken'd scene,
Some glittering ray of Hope there'll be,
 Where all in Sorrow's shade has been ;
And, radiant as that bird of blue,
 'Twill lighten up each darkest spot ;
But brighter, in its heavenly hue,
 Than bird or blue forget-me-not !

MISLETOE MORNING.

'Twas Misletoe morning,
And chanticleer's warning
Had summon'd fine folks from their beds and their
blankets,
When I saw, in a vision
Of Dreamland elysian,
A bevy of Cupids swarm forth for their prankets.

There was fun in their faces,
As all took their places,
And link'd themselves laughingly—mad little fro-
lickers!
And never such laughter
Shook roof-beam and rafter,
As shook the fat sides of these roystering rolickers!

With unfetter'd actions,
They form'd in two factions,

And, nude as old statues, selected their places :
> Little rosy carousers,
> Without any trousers,
And quite independent of straps and of braces !

> Such tints were their limbs on,
> Such hues of rich crimson,
Such roses and lilies, wax-apples and cherries,
> That they gleam'd hot and sunny,
> As, with frolickings funny,
They snowball'd each other with misletoe berries !

THE FOLK-LORE OF A COUNTRY PARISH.

Our country parish is quite a stronghold for superstitions, and most certainly does its best to preserve "the fast-fading relics of the old mythologies." It will not by any means get rid of its folk-lore fancies, but nourishes them with a tenderness that would be surprising to your fine men of the world and your sceptical dwellers in cities, who pooh-pooh our little idealities, and delight to amuse themselves with our marvels and mysteries. Let them do so, say I! It but little affects our parish, which goes on its way much as it did some scores of years ago—save that we have done with our witches, and no longer oblige our elderly females to sink or swim in the parish duck-pond.

But our country parish believes in many things that are not admitted into the creeds of the more enlightened towns. Permit me to divulge a few of the superstitious fancies that still abide with us : and believe me when I tell you that my tales are strictly true ones, and that their facts came within my own cognisance.

And first—which is beginning pretty nearly at the beginning—as to a baptismal superstition. It is not often that our parish church can produce more than one baptism at a time ; but, the other Sunday afternoon, there was the unusual number of three christenings— two boys and a girl. The parents of one boy were in a very respectable class of life : the parents of the two other children were in humble circumstances. The parties at the font had been duly placed by the officiating clergyman (Mr. Milkinsop, our esteemed curate) ; and, as it happened, the girl and her sponsors were placed last in order.

When the first child—who was the boy of the poor parents—was about to be baptized, the woman who carried the little girl elbowed her way up to Mr. Milkinsop, in order that the child she carried might be the first to be baptized. To do this she had (very contrary to the usual custom of the poor, who—in all essential points at least—are generally as refined as their superiors) rudely to push past her " betters "—*i. e.* the sponsors of the second boy. As she did so, she whispered to one of the sponsors, by way of apology :—

" It's a girl, so it *must* be christened first ! "

And christened first it was. But the peculiar manner in which this was brought about, showed that the woman was influenced by some peculiar feeling : and, on the next day, an opportunity was taken to discover her motive.

This was her explanation.

" You see, sir, the parson baint a married man, and consequentially is disfamiliar with children, or he'd never a put the little girl to be christen'd after the little boys. And, though it sadly fluster'd me, sir, to put myself afore my betters in the way which I was fossed to do, yet, sir, it was a doing of a kindness to them two little boys in me a setting of my little girl afore 'em."

" Why so ? " it was asked.

" Well, sir ! I *har* astonished as *you* don't know," was the reply of this specimen of our country parish. " Why, sir, if them little boys had been christen'd afore the little girl, *they'd* have had *her* soft chin, and *she'd* have had *their* hairy beards—the poor little innocent ! But, thank goodness ! I've kep' her from that misfortin' ! "

And the woman really believed that she had done so ; and, moreover, the generality of her neighbours shared her belief.

So let this fragment of folk-lore from our country parish prove a warning to clergymen—more especially to bachelors like Mr. Milkinsop—who would desire to stand well in the opinions of their poorer neighbours.

If twins are born in our country parish, it is believed that of the little bipeds—like the quadrupedal martin-heifers and free-martins—only one will prove the father (or mother) of a family.

If any of our women are seen abroad, and pursuing their ordinary out-of-door occupations, before they have been "churched," they at once lose caste in the eyes of their neighbours.

On the subject of marriage we have also our little peculiarities. Not a maiden in our parish will attend church on the three Sundays on which her banns are proclaimed. And this, not from bashfulness or mock-modesty; but because they deem such a proceeding to be eminently unlucky. When Mr. Milkinsop once asked one of these damsels what was the particular kind of ill-luck that she expected would have resulted from her attendance at church on those three particular Sundays, she informed the reverend gentleman that the offspring of such marriages would be born *deaf and dumb.* And, to clench this statement, and prove its truth by a forcible example, she adduced the instance of a young woman of her acquaintance who would

persist in going to church to hear her banns "asked
out," and whose *six* children were *in consequence* all
born deaf and dumb. No wonder, then, that our
village maidens stay away from church on those three
interesting Sundays, when such sad results are known
to follow a deviation from our country parish superstition.

Why or wherefore, when these young damsels present
themselves before Mr. Milkinsop to be united in the
bonds of wedlock to the husbands of their choice
they should carry a sprig of gorse as a bridal bouquet
is a mystery which I have been unable to solve. A
young lady fresh from school, and therefore well versed
in the mystical language of flowers, informs me that
gorse is an emblem of "enduring affection." I am
also aware of the old adage (for do we not use it in our
country parish, where the glorious gorse grows in such
large tracts that, when covered with its golden bloom,
it might induce a second Linnæus to throw himself
upon his knees and kiss the earth for producing flowers
so beautiful ?)—I am aware, I say, of the old adage
that says, "When the gorse is out of blossom, kissing
is out of fashion ;" by which is meant that kissing is
popular all the year round. But, still, I confess that
this adage and that emblem do not, as I believe, account for the appearance of the sprig of gorse in the

bridal bouquet, and that some further meaning lurks behind, which the damsels are unwilling should be brought to prominent notice. I therefore am constrained to leave this popular folk-lore where I found it.

The fine old church of our country parish has a pretty peal of bells, whose silvery tongues melodiously proclaim to the neighbourhood the various joyful events that break into pleasant ripples the still surface of our usual humdrum existence. The daughter of our chief farmer was married the other day, and, of course, the bells did their best to spread the tidings. The ringers rang when the bride and bridegroom left the church; and the ringers rang when the happy couple drove out of the parish in a chaise and pair for a honeymoon of four days in the great whirling world of London. And the ringers rang at divers times throughout the day, being filled with beer and friendly feeling. And, late in the evening, when the last peal had been rung, the ringers (according to the custom of our country parish) fore-*tolled* upon the great bell the number of children with which the marriage was to be blessed. This tintinnabular prophecy as to the "hostages to fortune" probably depends—like the gipsy predictions in similar cases— upon the largesse expected to be forthcoming. On this particular occasion, the clapper was made to smite the bell thrice three times. The bride and bridegroom, therefore, know the worst, and can betimes make the needful preparations for the advent of their tuneful nine.

All the young ladies in our country parish, in common with the young lady whom I have just mentioned, are imbued with the same superstitious spirit as their poorer neighbours. That leap-year empowers a young lady to " pop the question " to a young gentleman, is, I believe, a generally received fragment of folk-lore. But it is the belief of young ladies in our country parish, that leap-year permits them to do something more. I am informed by one of my fair young friends in that romantic village, that if, in any leap-year, she should so far forget herself as to suggest an union between herself and a bachelor acquaintance who should be uncivil enough to decline her polite proposals, she could, thereupon, demand from him the gift of a new silk dress : but that, to claim this dress with propriety, she must, at the time of asking, be the wearer of a scarlet petticoat ; which, or the lower portion of which she must forthwith exhibit to the gentleman ; who thereupon, by the law of leap-year—which is as the law of the Medes and Persians—is compelled to present to the lady a new silk dress, to cover her scarlet petticoat, and assuage her displeasure at his rejection of her proposals.

When my fair young friend told me this bit of feminine folk-lore, I laid it to heart, thinking that it might prove exceedingly useful to me, in putting me on my guard during the forthcoming leap-year. For, I thought within myself, that it was not without a determined significancy, that this young lady, and others in our country parish, had followed the then prevailing fashions (received by us a full twelvemonth after they have been introduced in more civilized places), and had habited themselves in bright scarlet petticoats—which, on a snowy day, and from beneath a looped-up dress, and over a pair of good, sensible legs, shod with good, sensible boots,—made, I can assure you, a great figure in the landscape, and, gleaming warm and sunny, presented to the eye that positive bit of colour which is so valuable to the artist. And I thought it might be reasonably inferred, that the ladies' law of leap-year was about to be inflicted upon the gentlemen of our country parish and the vicinity, in its most expensive silk-dress form, and that the assumption of these scarlet petticoats was merely the initiatory step to a sterner process.

And hence I thought that—from a careful consideration of the various dangers arising from this feminine folk-lore that would beset me, and all the other bachelors in our country parish, during the next twelvemonth,—I should be inclined to coincide with Mr. Meagle's opinion of beadles,* and to consider his advice with regard to those bipeds as worthy of all imitation; and so, when leap-year came, and when I caught sight of a young lady tripping along the road "in full fig," and displaying a scarlet petticoat, I should consider that I showed the best discretion by turning and running away.

When our Squire's daughter married Mr. Milkinsop's predecessor (who had been presented to a living) we subscribed for a testimonial to the bride and bridegroom. That to the bride, took the form of a silver cake-basket and knife; and when I presented it, on behalf of the parishioners, to the happy young lady, I was compelled (in obedience to their instructions) to demand from her a piece of money in return for the knife; for our folk-lore held, that to *give* a knife would "sever love and acquaintance." I need not say that the young lady laughingly complied with my request; and, now you know the history that attaches to the crooked sixpence that hangs from my watch-chain. And that crooked sixpence is in itself a piece

* See "Little Dorrit."

Y

of folk-lore; for **the wearing of it is considered to bring me " luck."**

We are great on the subject of the weather in our country parish. **In particular are we** attached to **prognostications of rain. If** the salt is damp, we say that we shall soon have wet. If we see a snake gliding and wriggling **across** the road, we say " there **will be rain before long." If we sec the** glow-worms shining at night, we say, "we shall have **wet ere morning." If we hear the woodpeckers** utter their peculiar, harsh **cry, we** say "we shall have a shower soon." We find our barometers in **all these things,** and many more ; **and, for us, the moon** " takes up her wondrous tale" chiefly to tell us what sort of weather it will be. **We say that "it will be a wet month, when there are two full moons in it."** Intending to **burst into immortal verse, but failing at the threshold in our search after a rhyme, we say,—**

> A Saturday's change, and a Sunday's full,
> **Once in** seven years is once too soon.

But we are more successful in our rhymes, when we treat of the gardening operations for spring. Then we say,—

> When elm leaves are as big as a shilling,
> Plant kidney-beans, if to plant 'em you're willing ;
> When elm leaves are as big as a penny,
> You *must* plant kidney-beans, if you mean to have any.

The energy infused into the last line, and the clearness of the advice contained in it, is a sufficient apology for its lengthened metre. In whatever quarter the wind may be on Candlemas-eve, our people say that it will "mainly" remain in that quarter for forty days. Concerning the unhealthiness of the spring season, we say,—

> March, search; April, try;
> May will prove if you live or die.

In regard to the approach of spring, we are not to be deceived. For we have a pretty saying, that the gentle season has not come in its "ethereal mildness," until we can plant our feet on twelve daisies. And when it is come, if you should chance to take violets or primroses into any of the houses in our country parish, I would warn you to be mindful to take not less than a handful of their blossoms; for less than this would bring certain destruction to the farmers' broods of young ducks and chickens.

Our fine old church keeps up the custom that was prevalent in the days of good George Herbert, and "at great festivals is strewed and stuck with boughs," like as was the church of "the country parson," or that of *Mr. Spectator*, where "the middle aisle was a very pretty shady walk, and the pews looked like so many arbours on each side of it." At Christmas it is decorated with holly and ivy; and mistletoe would be slily added, if Mr. Milkinsop were not preternaturally vigilant. On Good Friday it is dressed with solemn yew : and this, on Easter day, gives place to fresh boughs and primroses, and such spring flowers as may then have bloomed. Then, on Palm Sunday, we have palm-branches—that is, the nearest imitation thereto, in the shape of willow wands with their catkins and fluffy blanket-looking buds. And, on Whit-Sunday, we are brave with boughs and flowers.

There is no modern innovation in all this. The custom has been handed down to us from antiquity, and we take it as we found it. If any should class it among the " superstitions " of our country parish, surely it is a very simple and innocent one ! it is one, at any rate, with which our people would not willingly part; and one which they recognize with pleasure (not abusing it), while they bear in mind the sentence, " O all ye green things upon the earth, bless ye the Lord; praise Him, and magnify Him for ever."

When any one dies in our country parish, the passing-bell is tolled. If you listen to its solemn tongue, you may know the sex of the departed. Three times three for a woman; three times two for a man. As the last toll dies away in faint vibrations, the labourer out in the fields who hears it, bares his head, and says,

"God give him a good God-speed." This word "God-speed" is one of our country parish sayings. It means "the leaving one's house, in order to remove to a new home;" and they use it when they change from one dwelling-place to another.

It is not the custom to toll the passing-bell for a child that dies unbaptized. Was there more of love or superstition, in that young mother's heart, who came to the parson of our country parish, beseeching him with earnest pleadings that the passing-bell might be tolled for her dead and unbaptized little one, and so give rest to its soul? For she fancied that until the church-bell had tolled, her child's soul would be caged in unquiet rest in its dead body.

When a funeral approaches the church of our country parish, the solemn tolling is ceased, and a peal is rung. It has a melancholy sweetness that is very touching.

As a matter of course, the old superstition about the north side of the churchyard being under the dominion of evil spirits, has full sway in our country parish ; and not a funeral ever takes place in that portion of our "God's acre," or has been known to take place within the memory of our oldest inhabitant. I must except, though, that story he loves to tell, of having passed the churchyard in the dead of the night, once in the days of his youth, when he and poaching were more intimate than they ought to have been,—and being attracted by a light on the ghostly side of the churchyard,—and being overcome first by fear, and then by curiosity,—and then quietly stealing to the spot, and beholding by the flickering light of a lantern, a coffinless body being committed to the ground by two men,—and how he recognized them, and knew that the corpse was that of a woman who had been ruined and deserted, and in her despair had destroyed herself by poison. But this is an exceptional case; and the north side of our churchyard is, as yet, free from grassy mounds and hoary headstones.

Yet does this remind me of another funeral of which the same person has told me. Our country parish is a favourite resort of the gipsies. There is plenty of grass in the green lanes for camping purposes; and the brooks are very convenient. Our hedges suffer from the intrusion; but our hen-roosts and more valuable articles are safe; for our gipsies are grateful; and, after their own peculiar code of honour, thieve from our neighbours instead of from us. When a child is born to them, they bring it to Mr. Milkinsop to be baptized; and they themselves often come to church, and dazzle the eyes of our rustics, with handkerchiefs and waistcoats as gaily coloured as the stained-glass figures in the East window. In fact, a distant likeness might be traced between the two. Perhaps, the old parish-clerk may have reasoned this out for himself in his own peculiar fashion, and have come to associate those figures of Moses and Aaron in the painted window, with certain people whom he had both seen and known. For once, when a visitor to the church asked him if this particular window was not erected to the memory of Mr. and Mrs. So-and-so, the old man replied, as he pointed to the Moses and Aaron, —

"Yes, sir; but they don't much fature the old couple!"

But I am digressing from my gipsy, and the narrative of his death and burial, as told me by our oldest inhabitant. This gipsy was an ordinary member of his tribe, and he lay ill of a pleurisy, in the camp in our country parish. They called in a surgeon from the neighbouring town; and, after much persuasion, the surgeon bled him. The man became worse; the surgeon's assistant came to see him, and proposed to bleed him again. But the gipsies were much averse to blood-letting; so they sent the assistant about his business, paid the surgeon's bill, and dispensed with his further services. The man then died. He had expressed a wish to be buried in his best clothes, which were a velveteen coat with *half-crowns* shanked for buttons, and a waistcoat with *shillings* similarly shanked. But, his wish could not be carried out, as these valuable garments were stolen by a woman with whom he had lived, who forthwith decamped with her pilferings, leaving the gipsy to be buried in his second-best, without a shroud, in the very best of coffins.

"At the funeral," said my informant, "they had a hearse, and ostrich plumes : and about fifty gipsies, men and women, followed him ; and when the church service was over, and the clergyman was gone, the gipsies stayed behind in the churchyard, and had a service of their own. And, when a gipsy dies, you must know, sir, that they always burn everything belonging to him. First, they burnt his fiddle : a right-down good fiddler he was, and many's the time I've danced to him at our wake. And then they burnt a lot of beautiful Witney blankets, as were as good as new. And then they burnt a sight o' books, for he was quite a scholerd—very big books they wos, too ! I specially minds one on 'em— the biggest o' the hull lot ! a book o' jawgraphy, as 'ud tell you the history o' the hull world, you understand, sir ; and was chock full o' queer, out-landish picters. And then, there was his grinstun, that he used to go about the country with, a grindin'

scissors and razors, and sich like : they couldn't burn
him ! so they carried him two miles, and then hove
him right into the river. That's true, you may take
my word for it, sir ! for I was one as help'd 'em to
carry it."

But to return to our own peculiar folk-lore.

There is a sanitary superstition in our country
parish, which Mr. Milkinsop denounces as one of the
latest passages from the farce of Folly, and has dra-
matized thus :—

SCENE.—*The back premises of a Farm-house. Female domestic
plucking the feathers from a half-killed hen, which is writhing
with pain. Enter her Mistress, who expresses disgust at the
foul proceeding.*

MRS. Good gracious, girl ! how *can* you be so cruel ? Why,
the hen isn't dead !

DOM. No, mum ! I'm very sorry, mum ; but—(*as though answer-
ing a question*)—I was in a hurry to come down, and I *didn't* wash
my face this morning.

MRS. (*with rising doubts as to the girl's sanity in reference to her
sanitary proceedings.*) Wash your face ! Whatever does the girl
mean ? I did not say anything about washing your face. I said—
(*shouting to her, on the sudden supposition that she might be deaf*)
—that you were very cruel to pluck a hen that you've only half-
killed.

DOM. (*placidly.*) Yes, mum ! I'll go and wash my face directly.

MRS. (*bothered.*) Wash your face ? Yes, you dirty slut ! it
wants washing. But first kill this poor thing, and put it out of its
misery.

DOM. (*confidentially.*) I can't, mum, till I've washed my face.

MRS. (*repressing an inclination to use bad language.*) Why not ?

DOM. (*with the tone of an instructor.*) La, bless me, mum !
Why, don't you know as you can't kill any living thing till you've

washed your face first? I'm sure that I tried for full ten minutes
to wring this 'En's neck, and I couldn't kill her nohow. And all
because I hadn't time to wash my face this morning.

> [*The mistress administers a homily to the domestic ; the hen is
> put out of its misery, and the scene closes upon the domestic's
> ablutions.*]

Our country parish holds the same bit of folk-lore
with regard to the killing of pigs; so that when we
wish to slay our favourite porkers and Dorkings, the
commonest feelings of humanity lead us first to as-
certain if the executioner has washed his face.

In some places, people will turn their money when
they first see the new moon, in order to ensure a full
purse. But in our country parish, we say, that if we
eat pancakes on Goody Tuesday, and grey peas on Ash
Wednesday, we shall have money in our purse all the
year. It is Shrove Tuesday that we call by the name
of Goody, or Goodish Tuesday; and Mr. Milkinsop
inclines to the idea that this name is a rustic record of
the shriving and confession customary to the day prior
to the Reformation.

When the Autumn has come with its corn, and fruit,
and hops—for ours is a hop-growing parish, and our
folks have a saying "Plenty of lady-cows, plenty of
hops!" and like to see the pretty-spotted, and un-
pleasantly-scented insect ·that feeds on the destructive
aphis of the hop-plant—when autumn has come, and

the brown and reddened leaves are whirling down upon
the green meadows, the cows feed upon these sere and
yellow leaves, and thus give a bitter flavour to their
milk, and render it unfit for keeping, and this is why
folk-lore poetry says,—

> Farmers' wives! when the leaves do fall,
> 'Twill spoil your butter, and milk, and all!

We are old-fashioned people in our country parish,
and some of us have not yet fairly settled down into the
new style of reckoning the days and months of the
year, and it is not every one of us whose education is
sufficiently advanced to enable him to decipher Old
Moore's Almanack—notwithstanding that we make a
religious point of purchasing it, and frighten ourselves
on winter's nights by poring over its *Vox Stellarum*,
and its terrible hieroglyphic, where the pope is always
so uncommonly busy, and a royal coffin is perpetually
prepared. When we want to determine the question
between the old and new style, with regard to old
Christmas-day, our folk-lore formula is rather dangerous and costly to carry into execution; for, we say,
that if you throw a shovel-full of hot coals upon the
table-cloth, they will not burn it, if it is really old
Christmas-day. Though, I should think that the
table-cloth runs as great a risk of being destroyed as
did the poor old woman, who, two centuries ago, was

flung into our village pond, to see whether she was a witch or no. If she sank, and was drowned, she was considered innocent; but, if she floated, she was deemed guilty, and was put to death. Mr. Milkinsop has shown me in our church register, a memorandum of this witch-swimming, duly attested by the signature of the churchwardens. Happily for the old woman, she sank; and so ended her troubled life, without enduring fresh tortures, and, by this stroke of policy, triumphantly established the innocence that was now useless to her.

And this mention of Christmas, and of the old and new style, reminds me of what one of our farmers' wives told me of the curious circumstances attendant upon the death of her father. He was taken ill about Christmas-time. One night, he dreamed—or, to use his own words, "he awoke, and saw two men fighting together at the foot of his bed, one of whom told him that he would die on the ensuing thirteenth of March. In the morning, he related this to his family; and both he and they made light of it. Shortly after this he recovered; and, when the thirteenth of March came, he was, to all appearance, in good health. On the evening of that day he referred to his dream, and observed, 'I have done the ghost!'—'Don't be too sure of that,' said a foolish woman who was present;

'it's the New Style now, and ghosts don't know anything about it. They always go by the Old Style.'"
And this village oracle told him, that it would not
really be the thirteenth of March (by the ghost's
calendar) for twelve days to come. The farmer laid
this to heart; took to his bed, and died on the very
day predicted by the old woman, who, (notwithstanding that he ascribed his death to the ghostly warning)
would have met her deserts by a summary conviction
for manslaughter.*

The letting-in of the New Year is an important
matter in our country parish; though in our folk-lore
regarding it, we are not quite so polite as usual: for we
say, that if the first person who crosses your threshold
on the New Year's morning is a male, it will bring you
good luck through the ensuing year; whereas, if a
female is your first visitor, you will have bad luck.
Our carol-singers are up on a New Year's morning
before it is light, and strive who shall be first at the
various farm-houses. As soon as the inmates hear the

---

* Although this tale bears a certain degree of similarity to the
leading incident in the Lord Lyttelton ghost-story, yet I have not
the least doubt of its being thoroughly authentic; and it is here
told, as it was told to me by the daughter—a very respectable person, whose family had been well-to-do yeomen for two or three centuries. I may also remark, that all the other incidents and scraps
of folk-lore in this paper, have *really* fallen under my own notice
—though *not* within the bounds of the same "country parish."

song, they rise, and open the front door to admit the first lucky carol-singer into the house: they then conduct him through the house, and bow him out at the back door. You may be sure that he is not sent away empty: for, according to our folk-lore, he has brought good luck to that house for a whole twelvemonth. Of course, it is only the young gentlemen who are thus privileged to be the prognosticators of good luck.

Our farmers ought to be prosperous and well-to-do; for, as you see, they can ensure their yearly success on very easy conditions: and if they want to bring special good luck to their dairy, they take down the bough of mistletoe, and give it to the cow that calves first after New Year's Day. The cow devours it greedily; but sheep also do the same; and no wonder, if they like it. But the farmers ascribe the result to the mistletoe charm; and as their example sways those about them, it is not very wonderful that folk-lore should be found to flourish in our country parish.

THE CHRISTMAS TREE

AN ALLEGORY.

Heaven and Earth their prizes
   Have hung on the Christmas Tree;
All that man idolizes,
   There he can plainly see;
And Satan has more of the prizes,
   And most of the company.

Here are Sin's masqueraders—
   Wolves in the clothing of lambs—
In juggle and falsehood, traders,
   Dealers in cheats and shams.
      Onward they rush
      With a riotous crush;
And, so that they reach the Tree's fair fruit,
They care not the axe is laid to the root.

      Press on, ye rebel crew!
      The Prizes are all in view.

Avarice, Greed, and Fraud,
    Forget that ye are brothers !
Clutch at each glittering gaud—
    Mitre, and sceptre, and crown.
        Sword, and jewel, and star,
            Dangling above you they are;
Climb for them, tear them down !
    Why should you leave them for others?

Pride, and Power, and Place,
    Vanity, Vice, and Ambition,
    Gluttony, Envy, Sedition,
Race for the prizes, race !
Fight, and jostle, and grapple !
        Climb unto every shoot
        Hung with the world-sought fruit;
Pluck at each Dead Sea apple,
Whose golden rind so temptingly flashes.
    Bah ! 'tis an old wife's tale to a child,
To talk of their hollowness, shams, and ashes !
    By fables be never beguiled.

From the precipice ne'er heed the danger ;
    Ne'er pause to ponder and think,
How terribly nearsome and fearsome
    Is that yawning Pit's horrible brink.

Scale it with plank and ladder :
    Self is all your concern !
    Let the hot wine of Passion burn
Your hearts, and make them madder !—
  Ah ! would that it made them sadder.

You may clutch at the money-bags, miser,
  But, gold will not buy off your fate
Fool ! of Poverty thou art despiser,
  Who art poorer than Poverty's state !

You may beat your white bosoms, frail daughters,
  But, that calm-looking, passionate breast
  Throbs wild as the sea in unrest ;
Doves of Peace brood not over such waters.

Ah ! would that ye look'd above you
  To the Babe in the stable cave !
With a boundless love He doth love you ;
  In the greatness of might He can save.

Clutch not at the branches rotten,
  Though their fruit is so fair to see ;
Look at the bough He hath gotten,
  And the prize that He holdeth for thee !

No scathing lightnings blanch
That goodly, righteous Branch ;
Fresh and bright is its verdure ever,
Like the Gospel promise that dieth never.

Look on that Branch with eager eyes;
Bravely contend for its high-call'd prize.
For you, is balanced the weight of evil ;
But, you scorn to look
To the Saviour's Book,
And rush to the side, where the Devil
Looks down, with a grim delight,
On his children's maddening revel
On their chosen Christmas night.

For, Satan has hung his prizes
On the goodly Christmas Tree ;
And there, in Sin's disguises,
Crowd the thoughtless company.

MISSES OF MODERN LITERATURE.

SOME of the Misses of modern literature are misses in every sense of the word. They are living errors, who have mistaken their vocation, and have missed the mark at which they aimed. But there are Misses, and misses. There are some who were born, as it were, with the goose-quill in their fingers; and there are others who were born geese, and have taken up the quill from mistaken motives. To some of our literary misses, writing comes as naturally as eating and drinking; to others, it is as a stimulant, a bitter cup, or a forced draught. "To be a well-favoured man," said Dogberry, "is the gift of fortune; but to write and read comes by nature." And it has also been remarked that a poet is born and not made.

A great deal is said now-a-days concerning Woman's Work (always in double capitals), Woman's Sphere, Woman's Duty, and the like; and the great social problem of Woman has caused a vast deal of unneces-

sary thought and scheming in the breast of Man,
whose best way to solve the problem would be to
marry Woman off-hand, and not to ransack his brains
as to her manner of education, her sphere of duties,
her intellectual condition, or her social status. But,
while Man is pondering over the problem, Woman is
obliged to be up and doing; and, amongst other
methods of preserving herself from a merely vegeta-
tive existence, she has, of late years, taken to herself
the consolations of her pen, and found it to be always
an agreeable, and oftentimes a remunerative companion. Whether it be that the introduction of the
penny-post system has given to fluent young ladies a
hundred-fold power of indulging in that pleasant, gos-
siping letter-writing, in which they so greatly excel
over male correspondents; or whether it be that the
extension of the railroad system has similarly developed in travelling maidens a passion for jotting down
in journals and diaries their first impressions of novel
places and faces; or whether it be that the spread of
circulating libraries, and the creation of such institu-
tions as "Mudie's" or "Hookham's" have thereby
fostered a growing passion for, in the first place, reading, in the second place, weaving, and, in the third
place, writing romances; whether or no the travellers'
iron roads pave the way for the author's steel pens, or

the writing of gossip insensibly leads to the composition of larger works of fiction,—from whatever cause the effect may arise, it is very certain that never did literature boast of so many vestal votaries as at the present day. Pope's " mob of gentlemen who write with ease," are now very fairly matched by a bevy of fair ones, who are certainly matchless so long as they remain unmarried. Indeed, in looking over the long list of our misses of modern literature, we are constrained to ask, Why *are* they still misses? Why are they still dubbed by that mademoiselle prefix, which, if it had been addressed to a virtuous young lady in the days of the Merry Monarch, would have stigmatized her in the grossest manner? Why don't they get married? or *are* they married, although, like other professional *artistes*, they retain their maiden names when they come before the public? One would suppose that this was really the case with many of our literary misses, and that they were but surreptitious spinsters, after all, or how could they write so powerfully and naturally on the many tender secrets pertaining to courtship and marriage? To build up a truthful creation solely with fictitious materials, is the labour of no ordinary person; and the Miss Brontës who can create Mr. Rochesters are spinsters as exceptional as extraordinary.

However, we will dismiss all ingenious speculations on these points, and will leave our misses where we found them—which was, on the title-pages of their works; and, as we run our eyes over them, we are inclined to think that we have at least discovered that Woman's Work must mean printed works by women. They write about everything under the sun; they are historians, poets, novelists, botanists, archæologists, travellers, cooks, and female parsons: and, various as are their pursuits and accomplishments, yet, regarding them as a whole, and as an important class in our body politic, we may confess, with just as much truth as gallantry, that they have done good service to the State, and, by instruction and amusement, have delighted, soothed, informed, and charmed,—have been pleasant companions and ministering-angels,—and have done *their* parts in making themselves indispensable to man.

We imagine that no other country than Great Britain could produce, among their misses of modern literature, so many eminent names as those of Miss Evans, Miss Yonge, Miss Sewell, Miss Muloch, Miss Manning (authoress of "Mary Powell") Miss Martineau, Miss Strickland, and many other names, some of which are scarcely less important, and at which we will now glance under their respective departments.

In History, we may name Miss Agnes Strickland, our queen of lady historians, her sister, Miss Jane Strickland, Miss Freer, Miss Pardoe, Miss Emily S. Holt, Miss Corner, Miss Elwin, Miss Atkinson, and Miss Costello. Some of these daughters of Clio also claim to be ranked among our novelists, tourists, and tale-tellers: and are of kin to those who weave fact and fiction into the form of the historical novel, as Miss Manning has done in so many of her tales, and as Miss Gillies has also done in her civil-war tale of "The Carews." And claiming a Scotch cousinship with Clio, are those who edit historical biographies, like Miss Raikes, who has published her father's correspondence with the Duke of Wellington; or Miss Innes, the compiler of "Lodge's Peerage and Baronetage;" or Miss Jane Williams, the author of "The Literary Women of England;" or Miss Sarah Williams, who deciphered old manuscripts, and edited them for the Camden Society.*

In Social Science, we have the names of Miss Mar-

* Alas! that we should have to speak of Miss Williams in the past tense; but, ere the recently-published "Letters written by John Chamberlain during the Reign of Queen Elizabeth" could be placed in the reader's hand, Death had claimed the accomplished editor for his own; and the sunny, kindly, and studious Sarah Williams had sunk under her labours, and, at the early age of 33, had fallen a victim to that fell disease, consumption. Her carefully-edited work will be her best literary monument.

tineau, Miss Meteyard ("Silverpen"), Miss Carpenter, Miss Ann Blackwell, Miss Bessie Raynor Parkes, Miss Emily Shirreff, Miss Twining, Miss Frances P. Cobb, and Miss Nightingale; to which we might add the names of Miss Emily Faithfull and her coadjutor Miss Rye.

Of our Novelists, we have already mentioned some illustrious maiden names. To these we must add the names of Miss Marsh, of "Hedley Vicars'" fame, Miss Julia Addison, Miss Cuyler, Miss Marguerite Ann Power, Miss Augusta Johnstone, Miss Anna Harriet Drury, Miss Catherine St. Clair, Miss Grace Aguilar, Miss Frances Browne, Miss Palmer, Miss Goodrich, Miss Julia Corner, Miss Symonds, Miss Mary C. Hume, Miss Julia Kavanagh, Miss Frances M. Wilbraham, Miss Jewsbury, Miss Planché, Miss Susan Pitt, Miss Bowles, Miss Taylor, and others of whose maiden or married state we are doubtful, and whom, therefore, we are afraid to include in our list, lest we should err similarly to the *Saturday Review*, when (in its number for December 29, 1859), it pronounced Miss M. Betham Edwards to be a gentleman. But there are other Misses of modern literature who have penned fictions not only for amusement but for instruction. There are Miss Anne Bowman, Miss Ann Fraser Tytler, Miss M. Louisa Charlesworth, Miss

Emilia Marryatt, and the authoress of the "Tales of Kirkbeck." And this reminds us that the authors of "Dorothy," "A Trap to Catch a Sunbeam," "Aggesden Vicarage," and "My Life, by an Old Maid," are all said to belong to the school of Spinsters.

But of Spinsters of Song we have the names of many undoubted misses; Miss Proctor, Miss Isa Craig, Miss Braddon, Miss Winkworth, Miss Hume, Miss Eliza Cooke, Miss Gerda Fay, Miss Mitchell, Miss Marguerite Ann Power, Miss Macready, Miss Frances Browne, and Miss Christina Rosetti.

Among our Young Lady Travellers, we may name the following "unprotected females": Miss Selina Bunbury, the Misses Dunlop, the Misses Catlow, and Miss Emily Beaufort. And books of travels in connection with missionary labours have been published by Miss Barney, Miss E. Redgrave, and Miss Hughes.

Among Art-critics, Miss Theodosia Trollope and Miss Howitt must be honourably mentioned. Botany can boast of Miss Pirie, Miss Twamley, and the Misses Catlow. Zoology has Miss Mary Roberts; and Physical Geography Miss R. M. Zornlin, for exponents. Miss Marshall has translated Fénélon's Works; Miss Acton and Miss Esther Copley have displayed their skill in Cookery; and Miss Mary C. Hume has published her "spiritual" explanations of obscure texts of Scripture.

. Thus it will be seen that the Misses of modern literature are many in number, and that they can boast of names which rank among those of the leaders of the world of letters. Their worldly riches and positions are probably as various as the themes of their works ; for literary labour, even where it is crowned with success, is not always followed by wealth ; and fame and a full purse do not necessarily travel together. This, however, is a point on which we would not touch ; nor, out of idle curiosity, would we desire to lift the curtain that shrouds the sanctity of the literary maiden's private life.

THE TORCH-SPEECH.

Ἡφαιστος Ἴδης λαμπρὸν ἰκπιμπῶν σίλας.—ÆSCH., Ag. 270–305.

'Twas Vulcan was the messenger! *he* fired the beam-
   ing light!
The streaming flame from Ida came, and blazed upon
   its height;
And Ida sent the warning on to the Lemnœan steep,
And quick upon Mount Athos' top the burning fire
   did leap;
Then, on the surging ocean's back, the kindling flame
   of pine,
With ruddy blaze, like some sun's rays, all gleamingly
   did shine!
Quick, quick o'er-leaping ocean's waves, on went the
   speeding lamp!
The watchman of Macistus saw, as he his round did
   tramp:
He linger'd not, but sent it on; and soon the light
   did gleam
From such a self-same beacon flame, back from Euri-
   pus' stream.

The watchman of Messapius saw the glittering signal
    burn,
And spread the light by kindling bright a heap of
    wither'd fern.
From Azop's plain, the blazing torch, in brightness
    noway dimm'd,
Unto Cithæron's rugged steep, like dancing moon-
    beams, skimm'd:
Torch blazed to torch! fire answer'd fire! the kindling
    beacons burn;
And, through the night, the far-sprung light the wake-
    ful watch discern.
Gorgopis' darken'd waters then reflect the crimson
    light;
With rapid force, it speeds its course to Ægiplanc-
    ton's height:
High o'er the steeps, from peak to peak, it flashes high
    and higher,
Until the mountain-range becomes one streaming
    beard of fire!
The frowning crags that, towering, rise o'er the Saronic
    stream,
T' Arachne's height then hurl the light, like the lurid
    lightning's gleam;
Till Argos sees the beacon-blaze that Ida had begun,
And knows, with joy, that mighty Troy is captured
    and is won!

A WISH.

As the streamlet in its flow,
Smoothly gliding, calm and slow,—
Not dashing into sight
With the rapid river's might,—
Not unseen, yet, like the brook,
With an unobtrusive look,—
Ever onwards, slow but sure,
Making progress, bright and pure,—
Oh ! thus my life should pass !
Thus I'd have my life to pass.

Through the blossom'd banks of grass,
Where the nun-like violet grows,
There my brooklet ever flows
O'er its gleamy, pebbly bed ;
While, through the boughs o'erhead,
Dart the merry sunbeams bright,
In a golden shower of light ;

And, where lime trees dip their boughs,
There the lovers pledge their vows,
As they gaze into thy stream,
Dear brook, and see the theme—
The darling, pleasant theme—
Of young love's happiest dream.

I would live not like the ocean,
In boisterous commotion ;
Nor desire, like the river,
To go whirling on for ever ;
But would flow as tranquilly,
Dear brook, through life, as thee.

LITERARY AND ARTISTIC
PROFILES.

THE valuable labours of the American traveller Catlin had well-nigh been brought to an unexpected end from the mere fact of his painting a portrait in profile. His sitter was an Indian chief, of an unsophisticated nature, and with limited ideas as to the æsthetics of art. The red man knew that he had duplicate cheeks, eyes, nostrils, and ears; and he perceived that the pale-face had fixed him on the canvas with only half his possessions. With the logic of a savage, he therefore concluded that the one side of his countenance had been charmed away by the painter, who barely saved his life by daubing out the profile, and repainting the irate chief in " full face." This was an instance of a profile not meeting the requirements of an untutored nature.

Take an example to the contrary. Why do all the extant portraits of **Cardinal Wolsey** represent him in profile? There are the portraits in oil in the Halls

of the London College of Physicians, and Christ
Church College, Oxford; and there is the portrait in
stone over the portals of the latter building. These
are the most authentic likenesses of the " butcher's
dog " of " greasy genealogy;" and they, and less
authentic portraits, one and all, represent him in profile. A " full-face " portrait of Wolsey is not known.
Were these profiles the result of mere chance? By
no means. The Cardinal's contemporary, John Skelton, lets us into the secret; and, though so bitter
a satirist, yet we may credit him in this, for his statements agree with popular tradition, and satisfactorily
explain the profile portraits.

It seems, then, that the magnificent Cardinal, with
all his splendour of appearance, and gorgeousness of
apparel, was condemned to appear before men " with
a flap afore his eye;" and this (if Skelton and tradition speak truly) was the result of circumstances by
no means to his credit. When Mr. Charles Kean
played *Wolsey*, he judiciously omitted this veritable
eye-sore; although, with scrupulous fidelity, he dressed
the character to the minutest detail, and wore the iden-
tical hat that had covered the Cardinal's head in the
famous Field of the Cloth of Gold.

We do not wonder at a man like Wolsey, who
was so proud of his personal appearance, being very

chary of showing his disfigured side to the artist, who
was handing down his features to posterity. In this
respect, Wolsey was but an imitator of Hannibal, who,
says Mandeville, " had but one eye, though a flattering
limner painted him with both. This, Hannibal dis-
liked; but was very well pleased with another who
drew him in profile, an ingenious way of hiding a
man's blind side, without offending truth."

Now, we may see the counterpart of all this in Literature. While some writers will designedly falsify facts,
by giving their hero two sound eyes in place of one,
others will take a partial, one-sided view of his character, and will either keep his blind side entirely out of
sight, or will turn his worst side to us, and depict
him, as the satirist did the Cardinal, "with a flap afore
his eye." The literary profile-painters are a numerous
race, sometimes from choice, but more frequently from
necessity. It is so very much easier to hit off a portrait
in profile, than to truthfully represent the lineaments
of the full face! The one bears the same relation to
the other, that the clever profile sketches of Count
D'Orsay do to the Nelly O'Brien of Sir Joshua
Reynolds or the Mrs. Graham of Gainsborough.

Most of us, doubtless, have our blind sides; and
happy is the man who has no disfiguring flap over
his moral character. We should be better pleased if

officious friends would refrain from pointing to our blemish, or staring at us on our ugly side; but, if we are to fill a page in history, we must expect to be scrutinized from every point of view.   Perhaps we may side with Wolsey and Hannibal, and prefer the profile; perhaps we may hold with the Indian chief, and aver that the profile (however skilfully pourtrayed) does away with half the truth.   But whatever may be the sitter's predilections, any way the duty of the literary portrait-painter seems clear.   He must side with the savage, and cast Hannibal and Wolsey to the winds. There are no half-measures for him if he wishes to fulfil his duty.   He must not turn the best side of his hero to the reader, and keep the worst out of sight. If he would do his work well and truthfully, he must give us both sides—bad and good—blind eye and seeing eye—flap side and sound side.   It may not be necessary to raise the flap, and expose the repulsive evidence of vice; but still, let us have the flap.

It is certainly true, that the same thing may be variously looked at by two witnesses, each credible by himself; and that their testimony shall be discordant, and yet not beside the facts. The fables of the Chameleon and the Knight's Shield sufficiently instruct us on this point.   But it is the duty of the writer, more especially the historian, to look at both sides before he forms his final opinion; to hear the evidence on either side, before he delivers his verdict. What then? may he choose between them, and say, the one side is wholly right, the other is altogether wrong—I will paint that which pleaseth me most? By no means; for then he paints a profile only, where the reader expects him to depict a full face; and if there is but a profile eternally presented to our view, we may reasonably conclude that there is a blemished or a fairer side kept out of sight.

How few are there who can look facts and characters in full face! What with *suppressio veri* with regard to the unsightly side, and falsification with regard to the one blind eye, how rarely does the historian hold the mirror up to nature! Whig and Tory, Romanist and Protestant, all give their own discordant versions of the self-same simple story. What with partiality and partisanship, they all prefer to paint a profile instead of the full face. The adversary is like the satirist Skelton, and deliberately draws attention to the blemished side; the partisan keeps the blemished side out of sight; the panegyrist converts the blemish into a beauty. Amongst them all, we have some difficulty in arriving at the truth, and can only do so approximately after a careful study of the various versions of the same story.

Lord Macaulay went so far as to say, that it was impossible for an English historian to be impartial. Perhaps he framed this dictum to meet his own case. Compare his work with that of Alison—the political predilections of the latter claim his history to be " His-Tory " version of the facts ; while the picturesque artifices of the former, denote his history to be " His-Story." Yet both are portraits ; only they are taken from opposite sides, and so, instead of being full-face likenesses, they are merely Literary Profiles.

SOCIAL SILHOUETTES.

THE anecdote of Catlin's Indians who would not be painted "side-face" for fear of their full-face being charmed away, has met with a curious pendant. The Emperor of the French commissioned an artist to paint certain pictures commemorative of the visit to Paris made by the Siamese Ambassadors, who were therefore requested to sit for their likenesses. They did so, and great was their dismay on discovering that some among them were represented in profile. They protested to the artist against the cruel wrong that he had done them in depriving them of one half of their facial property, and demanded that both sides of their faces should be depicted. It was replied to them, that the artistic grouping of the picture demanded that certain of the figures should be seen in profile, and therefore that their request could not be complied with. The difficulty was eventually surmounted by the protest of the Siamese, and their delivery of a written testimony (to be for ever preserved in the archives of France) that they had two sides to their faces.

If the requirements of the artist's canvas had in this instance been less peremptory, the request of the Ambassadors might more easily have been complied with than the demand of old Astley (of the Amphitheatre), who insisted that his scene-painter should represent a drum (in a picture of military trophies) so as to show its two heads. "But, sir," remonstrated the painter, "according to the rules of perspective, you could only see one head to the drum." "What have I to do with perspective?" replied the unlettered proprietor; "I pays you for painting, and not for perspective. Every drum in my establishment has got two heads, and with two heads it shall be painted." The painter pondered over his difficulty, and by the next time that his master inspected his work and asked him where was the other head of the drum, was enabled to answer, "It is behind the drapery of that trumpet:" a reply which was perfectly satisfactory to old Astley.

In these instances the untutored mind was not satisfied with a representation of half the truth. They had a pre-Raffaelite, no-fudge principle strong within them, and they required things to be represented as they appeared to their own eyes, regardless whether they looked right or **wrong, well or ill. In** all this, their rude logic made them **hit** upon the right scent, although **they could not correctly follow it up;** clutching at the **Will-o'-wisp of Truth,** they floundered into the **bog of Error. It is true** that they showed but little knowledge of the **painter's craft; but** it is also true that they had a **glimmering** of that stern faithfulness of Art which demands a **recognition of** opposites, and is not satisfied with one-sided representations; and, in this respect **at least,** partial historians, partizan writers, and **profile-painting authors, may learn a** lesson from the **savage.** These literary profilists are even surpassed **in number, no less** perhaps **than in** talent, by those **writers who devote themselves to the** production of Social Silhouettes—by which we mean those sketches of every-day life and character which may be broadly and forcibly hit off, and yet, after all, be one-sided representations, drawn from only one stand-point, and as different to the carefully-delineated "full-face" picture, **as a** *chef d'œuvre* of Reynolds would be to **the profile portrait** skilfully cut out of black paper with a pair of **scissors.**

At the present day the writers **of Social** Silhouettes form a numerous class, either from possessing some special talent that way, **or from** the popularity of the style itself, or from the ease with which it may be worked, or from that passion for what is usually termed "graphic writing," which has been so much fostered by the clever correspondents of the newspaper press. How far the production of Social Silhouettes ought to be carried, and whether they have more than a temporary and superficial value, are points on which the reading public are the best judges; so long as they demand them, we may feel assured that the supply will be maintained. It is undoubtedly the truth, that every person has traits of character more or less developed, and that the writer who would desire to represent any character with even approximate correctness of delineation, must study it from all points, and depict it with all its traits, bestowing equal attention on those less marked as well as on those strongly defined, and endeavouring to hold the mirror up to nature, so as to show both Virtue's feature and Scorn's image. But the artist whose forte lies in Social Silhouettes, does nothing of the kind; instead of studying his character from all sides, and looking at it in all ways, and probing it in all places, he merely seizes upon one or two leading characteristics, and hits them off in an easy touch-and-go style, usually throwing in a dash of caricature to mark the portrait more forcibly.

But why complain of this? It is all very well that the literary portrait-painter of historical characters

should not represent them in profile, but should show
us the blind sides of Hannibal and Wolsey, and give
us the unsightly with the pleasing, for this is the
duty of the faithful historian ; but with the scribbling
sketcher, *cui bono ?* why should it be demanded of him
also that he must give us the disagreeable side, when
he undertakes only to set before us that which is
agreeable ? If he does not falsify truth thereby,
and if it be an understood thing that he under-
stands his vocation, and when Social Silhouettes
are asked for, supplies them, and not the highly-
finished full-faced portrait—then, why should he
be blamed for devoting himself to a lower work of
Art, so long as it meets a public demand ? The archi-
tects of buildings that are to last for centuries, and
the putters-up of ornamental arches and pretty decorations, are both useful in their several ways, and can
perform their duties to themselves and to society in a
conscientious manner. If a person has neither the
time nor talent to paint a Sir Joshua, he may at least
creditably and usefully employ himself in producing
a Silhouette. There is a wide difference between the
black profile snipped out in a few minutes and the
portrait on which months of thought and consummate
Art have been bestowed ; and yet each may tell us for
whom the portrait was intended—although the one

simply does this, while the other denotes the mind
and character of the person represented.

There was, at least, one feature in common to the
Duke of Wellington, Sir Charles Napier, Ovid, and
Paulinus—whom Bede describes with a *naso adunco*—
which Wordsworth translates—

"His prominent feature like an eagle's beak ;"

.and while the Social Silhouette writer would have
seized upon the noses of these illustrious personages,
and caricatured them with an exaggerated breadth of
handling, the duty of the historian would have lain in
an opposite direction, and he would have left the nose
where he found it. The writer who stands on the
highest pedestal offers himself as the most notable
mark for the critic ; and Mr. Dickens has usually been
brought forward as a master in the art of producing
Social Silhouettes—as an author, that is, who individualizes his fictitious personages more by little outward
traits, and tricks and turns of expression, than by any
deep research into character or development of mind.
Mr. Carker's teeth, and Rigaud's moustache that went
up and nose that came down, are commonly adduced
as instances in point. This sort of thing (it is ob-
jected) certainly individualizes the character and helps
to stamp it upon the mind ; but it is a mere trick,

although a clever one. It is little better (the objectors go on to say) than the device of the farce writer,
who assigns to each of his *dramatis personæ* some
catch word or sentence, and by condemning them to
certain utterances, and keeping them in one groove, is
enabled to achieve his object at the least expenditure of
thought, but with a certain sacrifice to verisimilitude.

It is very clear that this class of objectors would
set little store by the Social Silhouettes of literature.
Nevertheless, although they do not pretend to a very
high rank as works of Art, they require no mean talent
or skill at their fabricator's hands—they keep him usefully employed in a work for which he may possess
special aptitude—and, blended with some instruction,
they provide harmless amusement for thousands of
toilers to whom happy thoughts and airy fancies are as
medicines to the mind. Many of the bright flowers
of literature are presented to us in the shape of Social
Silhouettes; and so long as they do not come before
us as useless or poisonous weeds, we may be glad to
welcome them, even if they are but as the shells picked
up on the shore, with which we amuse ourselves for a
few moments, and then fling to oblivion.

THE PRAISES OF COLONOS.

(Edip. Col. 668—719.)

———

Welcome, stranger ! thou hast come
To the gods'-well-favour'd home,
Where Colonos rears on high
Its chalky cliffs unto the sky ;
Listen, stranger, and I'll tell
All the joys that here do dwell !

Here are horses that with pride
E'en a king would deign to ride ;
Here the sweet-voiced nightingales
Softly tell their mournful tales,
Where the purple ivy's bloom
Shrouds the vale in twilight gloom !

Here's the leafy, pathless grove,
Which the Wine-god deigns to love,

Where the mighty trees have made
Gloomy aisles of unpierced* shade,
Where the tempest's raging breath
Stirs not e'en a leaf in death.†

Here, within the leafy halls,
Roam the joyous Bacchanals ;
The Nysian nymphs, who from the first
Never left the god they nurst,
But now with laugh and merry stir
Crowd around the Reveller !

Here, enrich'd by heavenly dew,
The golden crocus burst to view,
And the sweet narcissus throws
All around its clustering snows ;
The holy flower which erst, 'tis said,
Wreath'd a mighty goddess' head.

* " Where the *unpierced* shade
    Imbrown'd the noontide bowers."—*Milton.*

†   " No stir of air was there ;
Not so much life as on a summer's day
Robs not one light seed from the feather'd grass,
But where the dead leaf fell, there did it lie."—*Keats.*

Here the sleepless fountains ever
Stream into Cephissus' river;
Earth enriching in their flow,
Nomad-like, they wandering go,
Loved by all the Muses mighty
And by gold-rein'd Aphrodite.

Here I've heard, too, is a tree,
Such as Asia ne'er did see,
Unplanted by man's hand, the fear
Of friendly and of hostile spear :
For 'tis here the olive grows,
In the land where first it rose !

Here shall neither young nor old
E'er be impiously bold
To cut down the sacred grove,
For 'tis watch'd by Mysian Jove,
And the great Minerva too,
With her eyes of melting blue !

Here, (and this I reckon most
For the Mother-City's boast,)
Here, 'twas first the Ocean King
Bade the stately steed to spring,

And with bits did curb him then
To be useful unto men !

Thus our city's reach'd the height
Where true Glory sheds her light ;
She's the nurse of chivalry,
And the mistress of the sea ;
And 'tis thou, O Saturn's son,
That this mighty work hast done !

Dashing through the briny sea,
The tall ship bounds on wondrously,
Tracking through the waste of waters
Nereus' hundred-footed daughters :
For our King is Saturn's son !
Stranger ! now my tale is done !

SOMEBODY'S EYES.

WHILE yet I gazed, she woke : not suddenly,
 But slowly coming back to life,—as Venus might
Have risen from the foaming of the sparkling sea,
 And shaken from her hair the wave-drops bright,—
And then, as slowly, she unclosed her eyes—
  Eyes like unto the deepest hue
  Of Adria's waters " darkly blue,"
And not the pale cœrulean of the skies.

And what an ocean is a woman's eye !
  With bright thoughts ever floating through
  Its deepest depths of bluest blue,
Where, lurking at the bottom, Love doth lie !
And yet, those deep blue waters are so bright, so clear,
That you can see yourself reflected there !

MARELI;

OR, THE BEST WAY OF GETTING OVER A DIFFICULTY.

CHAPTER I.

WELCOME LITTLE STRANGER!

" What's in a name?"—*The Author of Shakspeare.*

" Being now in possession of a daughter, it became necessary to give her a name ; and nobody would believe the meditations, the consultations, and the comical discussions he held on this important point. At last he determined to *invent* one ; and, Saba was the result."— *Sydney Smith's Memoirs, Vol. I. p.* 22.

" No names are too absurd for parents to give their children. Here are innocents stamped for life as ' Kidnum Toats,' ' Lavender Marjoram,' ' Patient Pipe,' ' Talitha Cumi,' ' Fussy Gotobed,' and, strangest of all, here is one called ' Eli Lama Sabacthani Pressnail.' "—(*Curiosities of Registration. Chambers's Journal.*)

" It is all over, sir ; and it is all right !" said Mrs. Toosypegs, as she entered the breakfast-parlour, with a bundle of flannel in her arms.

Mr. Chickenhackle murmured something that sounded like a thanksgiving, as he wiped from his brow the beads of perspiration with which it was

bedewed.   Poor man ! he had been in a terrible state
of anxiety for some hours past, and had seen but little
of the columns of *The Times,* over which his eyes had
been dreamingly poring.   His thoughts had wandered
upstairs to his wife's bedroom, and had there remained,
until forcibly brought back by the monthly nurse.
She came before him with the mysterious manner of
her profession, and with the aspect of one who was the
bearer of good tidings.

"Yes sir !" observed Mrs. Toosypegs, making answer to herself, in the absence of any remark from Mr.
Chickenhackle ; " Yes, sir, it is all over ; and it is all
right."

"And Maria—Mrs. C.—is she—"

"As well as can be expected, sir," replied Mrs.
Toosypegs, "and will be able to see you soon.   But,
what I always says—and I've nussed parties enough to
know it—is this ; that gentlemen should not be *too*
anxious to see their ladies," (I wonder, by the way, if
any professional nurse could ever be induced to make
use of those two simple English words, husband and
wife !) "as it's apt to perdoose excitement, and throw
'em back.   If gentlemen was always content to wait
until we gave 'em permission, their ladies would get on
a deal quicker, and do us more credit."

The maxims of Mrs. Toosypegs were here cut short

by a sharp cry that proceeded from the bundle of
flannel borne in her arms.

"Why, what is that?" cried Mr. Chickenhackle,
in some astonishment, and but slowly awaking to a
realisation of the tremendous fact that he was a parent; "What is that?"

"That!" responded Mrs. Toosypegs, as she play-
fully plunged her fore-finger into the folds of flannel,
"Why, bless its little life, did it want to see its own
father, then?" You see, she replied, Quaker-like, by
putting a question in place of the answer.

"Its father!" stammered Mr. Chickenhackle,
though with a feeling of doubt as to whether her
words had been addressed to him, or to the flannel
bundle; "Then, have you got the child there?"

"The blessed babe is here, sir, and nowheres else,"
replied the nurse; "I thought you would like to see
it."

"Of course, of course! Bless me! and that is a
baby!" pondered Mr. Chickenhackle, as, with wonder
written upon his face, he raised his double eyeglass,
and scrutinized the contents of Mrs. Toosypegs'
bundle. "Bless me! and that is a baby! *the* baby!
MY baby!"

"It is to be hoped so, sir!" said Mrs. Toosypegs,
with a dubious cough.

"It is very—red!" said Mr. Chickenhackle, continuing his eyeglass scrutiny, without heeding the nurse's insinuation.

"You wouldn't have it black, sir, surely!"

"No; I prefer the *rouge* to the *noir*. But it seems odd that white people should be born with skins like Red Indians. Is it a boy or a girl?"

"A girl, sir; and as fine a little lady as I ever see. Equal already to a many at a month." It was a very remarkable fact, but so it was—at any rate, if her statement was to be credited—that every child, over whose honeymoon of existence Mrs. Toosypegs presided, seemed to be specially endowed by nature with extraordinary qualities, and miraculously advanced to physical proportions far greater than those with which the diminutive Lilliputian usually makes its appearance among its fellow Brobdignagians. It was as though—at least, she would have her employers believe it so—some special charm hovered around Mrs. Toosypegs, and brought good luck to her patrons. And, more remarkable still, the child last born was always the finest of the Toosypegs' series: so much so, that it seemed within the bounds of probability that the series would one day be developed into giants.

"A girl! ah, good! Though I could have wished it had been a boy," murmured Mr. Chickenhackle, still curiously inspecting through his eyeglass the lively little portrait, set in its frame of flannel. It was a stereoscopic portrait : in one picture, you had two combined. When you looked at the baby, you saw both the husband and the wife.

"It's better to have a girl the first time, sir," said the nurse, who always made a professional point of having her axioms ready for every emergency; "as there's an old saying,—

> "Girl first, and boy after,
> Brings good luck to roof and rafter."

Mrs. Toosypegs was never at a fault; "semper parata" may have been her motto as touching the maxims of a monthly nurse. If Mr. Chickenhackle's baby had been a boy, she would have said,—

> "Should their parents wish for joy,
> Let their first-born be a boy :"—

but, as it was, she reminded him of the other sagacious piece of folk-lore. There is not a proverb but what may be capped, and contradicted, by another proverb.

"Then I'll be satisfied with my good luck," said Mr. Chickenhackle. "But she must certainly not be called Blanche, if her complexion is to remain of this blushing hue. Rose would be more appropriate : not to say Pickled Cabbage. The organization of her lungs appears to be perfectly satisfactory; eh, nurse?"

"The organ what, sir!"

"Ah, well; never mind! a young lady's voice is musically termed an organ, and I must confess that this little lady's voice has less of the *piano* than the *forte,* and has more the power of the organ."

"Bless its little heart, then! tchk, tchk, tchk!" was Mrs. Toosypeg's reply to what she did not understand, as she endeavoured to quiet the child, who was doing its best to justify its father's description.

A short pursy man entered the room.

"Mr. C.," said the doctor, "I congratulate you, sir, on being the father of a very fine little girl. Mrs. C. is going on as favourably as we can expect; and I will allow you to see her for three minutes : for three minutes, and not a second more. Nurse, you can bring the child up-stairs."

"She must certainly be christened Rose!" murmured Mr. Chickenhackle, as he meekly followed the doctor and nurse, and gazed upon the rubicund face of his first-born.

CHAPTER II.

GODMOTHER NUMBER ONE.

"The name of Rose, my dear, would have been more appropriate seven days ago than it is now;" said Mr. Chickenhackle, a week after the "interesting" event just recorded.

His first-born, somewhat less rubicund as to the face, but more demonstrative in the exercise of her "organ," was lying in its mother's arms. Mrs. Chickenhackle was engaged in that most womanly of all occupations familiarly known as "nursing."

"Rose is a pretty name," said the Mamma; "but I think another one would be preferable."

"The Rose under any other name would smell as sweet;" chuckled Papa. "Let it be Maria, then. I am sure, my dear, I always thought your name a very pretty one when I was courting you. Don't you remember that I broke my penknife over it on that stile where I used to sit and watch for you. Ah! those were happy days!"

"Not happier than now, John, surely?" murmured Mamma in her sweetest voice, as she stole her thin white hand into her husband's.

Mr. Chickenhackle gallantly covered it with kisses. "Happier? no, not by one-thousandth part! I remember when I had to make a speech at our wedding-breakfast. I said that *that* day was the happiest day in my life. And perhaps it may have been up to that time. But, it was only the day that led up to my really happiest days; the gate that opened to the realms of happiness. To my thinking, my dear, the happiest days of married life are not known, until a third little personage makes its appearance upon the scene."

A tap at the door of the bedroom where this colloquy took place, interrupted Mr. Chickenhackle's eloquent oration on wedded bliss. The comer was his half-sister, Miss Ricketts, a maiden lady some twenty years older than himself, and much looked up to, and deservedly respected, as the owner of a very comfortable independence.

When a quarter of an hour had been consumed in the interesting inquiries that are usually made into the condition of infants and their mothers, Miss Ricketts observed, "I suppose you look to me, brother John, to be one of the little dear's godmothers?"

Brother John had looked at that very thing; and his mental glance had fallen upon his half-sister's property, a share of which she might, perhaps, be induced to leave to her niece and godchild. So he said, " It is both my own and Maria's wish that you should do us the favour to be one of the godmothers."

" And the other godmother ? " asked Miss Ricketts.

" Will be Maria's aunt, Miss Meagrim ; " answered brother John.

Now, there was not much love lost, as the saying is, between Miss Meagrim and Miss Ricketts. Both were ladies of a certain age ; both were possessed of independent property ; and both were excessively fond of displaying their power of wealth upon all occasions. If Miss Meagrim placed her name as a subscriber of one guinea to the " Charitable Society for providing Flannel Jackets for Sheared Sheep," Miss Ricketts forthwith contributed two guineas to the Society's funds. If the name of Miss Ricketts was published to the world as a donor of five pounds to " the Washerwomans' Dolly Club, and Soft-soap Distribution Society," Miss Meagrim's name was presently seen in advance of a donation of ten pounds. Each maiden lady endeavoured to out-trump the other. Each strove hard to obtain a more conspicuous seat in the Temple of Mammon. Each essayed to play first-fiddle in the social band of their town ; and it must be confessed that the local charities throve

thereby. When fools fall out, honest men come by
their own.

So Miss Ricketts, looking as though, if squeezed,
verjuice might be distilled from her, said, " Did my
ears deceive me, brother John; or did you observe
that Miss Mcagrim was selected for the other godmother ?"

Brother John corroborated his previous statement

" Oh ! " said Miss Ricketts.

Now, that little monosyllable " Oh," may be made
to express nearly every shade of feeling. Not even a
young lady's monosyllabic " No " may be so twisted
into an opposite signification. Sentiment, wonder,
fear, rage, diffidence, doubt, acquiescence, enthusiasm,
admiration, pain,—every phase of feeling may that
little interjection be made to express, simply by the
inflection of the voice.

Miss Ricketts' " Oh ! " was a dry " Oh ! " expressive
of displeasure.

" We thought we had better ask her, as she is my
aunt," observed Mrs. Chickenhackle.

" So that we might have the one godmother from
the father's, and the other from the mother's side;"
said brother John.

" Oh, certainly ! quite right ! " said Miss Ricketts,

in a tone that belied her words, and proclaimed that all was wrong. "And what name pray, brother John, do you propose to give to *my* niece?" She emphasized *my* with a plain reference to Miss Meagrim.

"Well, sister, we were talking about that when you came in, and we had scarcely made up our minds," said brother John.

"It is usual to name a female child after one of its godmothers," suggested Miss Ricketts.

"Or both!" supplemented brother John, anxious to bridge over the difficulty, whose yawning chasm he now descried near at hand.

"Just as you wish," said Miss Ricketts, with the air of one to whom all things are agreeable. "But, I must say, that I cannot see that two names are necessary for a child. None of our family, brother John, ever had more than one, and I think it would seem like an insult to our parents if you gave to your children more names than they thought fit to give to theirs."

"Well, I am sure I don't care a straw about having two names for the little roguey-poguey," returned Mr. Chickenhackle, with a sudden dart of obtrusive affection at the infant who was the unconscious cause of this discussion and difficulty; "so it shall only have one then—it shall, it shall!" And the fond parent whistled and chirrupped in the child's face, and waggled his head, and snapped his fingers, in his parental endeavours to attract the notice of his off-spring, who appeared to be devoting its leisure time to staring at nothing in particular upon the ceiling.

"Then that settles the matter at once!" said Miss Ricketts, judicially summing up the case. "So, you will name her Mary, after me?"

"We will—eh, Maria?"

"If you wish it, my dear; but I hope Aunt Elizabeth will not be offended."

"Not she!" said Mr. Chickenhackle (most rashly); "and if she is, why, she shall name the next! ha, ha, ha! eh, Maria?"

MARIA.—Don't, love! I can't bear to think of it.

MISS R.—He, he, he! Miss Meagrim may not have so very long to wait. Eh, my little god-daughter, Mary?

BABY (*removing its eyes from the ceiling, and fixing them intently on Miss R.*)—Ya haa! ya haa! ya haa!

MAMMA.—Oh, bless it, bless it! (*quiets it in the usual way.*)

[Scene closes.]

CHAPTER III.

GODMOTHER NUMBER TWO.

ONE hour after Miss Ricketts had left Mrs. Chicken-hackle's room, Miss Meagrim entered it. The wish was expressed, that she would be one of baby's godmothers in conjunction with Miss Ricketts.

"Of course, my dear Maria, I shall be most delighted," said Miss Meagrim; "nothing, I am sure, could give me greater pleasure; and you may depend upon it, that I shall be a good friend to my little god-child, and that, when I am removed from this wicked world," (here Miss Meagrim shut her eyes, and shook her head,) "her name shall be found in my will. And, between you and me," this was said with suggestive mystery, "I dare say, I shall do much more for her than Miss Ricketts will ever think of doing. But, I hear Mr. C.'s foot upon the stairs, so, out of deference to his feelings, I will say no more on that point. I will simply content myself with observing—Oh! here Mr. C. is."

"Oh, Miss Meagrim!" said Mr. Chickenhackle, pleasantly, bearing in mind the maiden's private property; "Oh, Miss Meagrim! come to see your little niece! or, as I should say, if I should speak correctly, your little *great*-niece: ha! ha! and I hope your god-daughter also? I suppose Maria has expressed to you our wish, that you would stand to the child?"

"To which I have already consented with the greatest pleasure," replied the maiden; "and I was observing, as you came in, Mr. C., that the sweet innocent shall never repent having *me* for a godmother." Miss Meagrim laid a great stress upon the *me*, as though to infer that the case was dubious with respect to the other godmother.

Mr. Chickenhackle perceived this, and commenced somewhat sternly with "Standing in the relationship to me that Miss Ricketts does—" but suddenly softened down, as he reflected upon the pecuniary benefit that his child might derive from Miss Meagrim being treated sponsorially and otherwise on the most agreeable terms—"of course, you see, my dear Miss Meagrim, we could do no less than ask her to act in conjunction with yourself."

"Oh, of course!" replied the maiden, with suspicious acidity of manner. "And the name—had you fixed upon that?" She asked this, as though it were a matter of perfect indifference.

"Why," said Mr. Chickenhackle, with some hesitation, "Maria—that is, I—we had certainly talked it over, and we thought that it would be best to—yes! to give it a name."

Maria was altogether taken up with her baby.

"Oh! you thought it best that it should have a name, then!" said Miss Meagrim, bitingly, scenting what was in the wind. "And what name, pray, may I ask, did you fix upon, Mr. C.?"

Mrs. Chickenhackle endeavoured to come to the rescue: "you have not told me, aunt, who you think baby is like. *I* think that her forehead and chin are like John's; but—" but it was of no avail; the *ruse* did not succeed.

"Was the name that you decided upon, Mary?" continued Miss Meagrim, plunging a stiletto look full into Mr. Chickenhackle's face.

"Well, now! bless my life, my dear Miss Meagrim," responded the unfortunate gentleman, "it was very extraordinary that you should guess the very word, wasn't it?"

"Very!" said Miss Meagrim, so drily, that it seemed as if it was an age since her tongue had been lubricated by the milk of human kindness.

"Yes: Mary was the name," went on Mr. Chickenhackle, in a hurried, nervous voice. "It was the name you know, of—of my grandmother; and my sister; quite a family name."

"Quite!" The want of the lubrication just referred to was really remarkable. "And so you name
the child after Miss Ricketts?" said Miss Meagrim,
though more with a note of intimidation than interro-
gation.

"Well! I don't altogether know about that," ob-
served Mr. Chickenhackle, fencing with the question.
"But, we certainly thought of calling her Mary; and
Mary does happen to be my sister's name."

"And you do not give the child a second name?"
pursued Miss Meagrim, with another stiletto look.

"No; we thought one would be enough," rejoined
her victim. "We are plain people, you know, Miss
Meagrim; and we don't much care about having more
names than we want. Sister Ricketts only wished one
name."

"Then the other godmother is not to be noticed?
I am to be passed over in favour of Miss Ricketts!"
Miss Meagrim's interrogatories were still in the form
of notes of intimidation.

"Oh, no! I am sure we didn't mean that!"

"Oh, dear no, aunt Elizabeth! nothing, I am sure,
could be further from our thoughts!" cried husband
and wife, in a breath.

"Then, why could you not name the child after
me?" (Another stiletto look.)

"Well!" said Mr. Chickenhackle—as many people say in dubious things, and matters of ill; "Well! I don't know that I have a passion for the name of Mary—ahem!—Byron. And certainly, Elizabeth is a fine name, my dear Miss Meagrim, and can be played upon more than any other name, perhaps; Lizzie and Liz, Bessy and Bess, Betty and Bet, for example."

"Then you can call the child Elizabeth, instead of Mary;" said Miss Meagrim, sticking close to her subject, like an Indian hunter to his trail, and not to be led away by improper remarks on proper names.

"Instead of?" faltered Mr. Chickenhackle. "Why you see—in fact—we promised my sister that the child should be called Mary."

"Oh, then! you *did* promise Miss Ricketts to name the child after her?" said Miss Meagrim, with the pouncing air of a barrister, who has been cross-questioning a reluctant witness, and has at last drawn forth the answer he was searching after.

"Ye-es!" faltered her victim.

"Oh!" said Miss Meagrim, very drily, lacking the afore-mentioned lubrication. "Then, Mr. C., in that case, as the child will not be called by my name, you cannot expect that I should do anything for her."

"I am sure, dear aunt," said the Mamma, "that we shall be excessively sorry if—"

"Oh! I will stand as godmother," interrupted Miss Meagrim; "but, surely, nothing more can be expected?" And the maiden lady threw herself back in her seat, and rapped her teeth with the handle of her parasol, as though she was knocking at the door of her lips to ask if anything more *could* be expected. It was clear that the answer would be unfavourable.

"Maria, my dear! Baby must have two names," said Mr. Chickenhackle, suddenly, but firmly.

"Certainly, John," replied his obedient spouse; "I am sure we would not displease aunt Elizabeth for the world."

"Baby must be called Mary Elizabeth!" said Mr. Chickenhackle.

"Excuse me!" interrupted Miss Meagrim, who, so long as she could help it, was not going to be placed second to Miss Ricketts even in such a matter as this; "excuse me! but baby must be called Elizabeth Mary; making Elizabeth come before Mary."

"She came after her in history," said Mr. Chickenhackle, with a dismal attempt at a joke.

"But was before her in reputation and popularity," rejoined Miss Meagrim, sharply, with another stiletto look.

"Miss Ricketts can have no objection I am sure!" confidently asserted Mrs. Chickenhackle.

Her husband and aunt thought otherwise, but said nothing.

"Mary Elizabeth, or Elizabeth Mary is all one," observed Mrs. Chickenhackle.

"Not quite!" said Miss Meagrim drily. "For, if it is Mary Elizabeth, I shall give baby a godmother's present of a silver knife and folk, or something of that sort : whereas, if it should be Elizabeth Mary, I will leave her ten thousand pounds. Either my name must come first, or the legacy must go to some one else. I have little doubt, but what I should be able to find hundreds of god-daughters on these conditions." And Miss Meagrim again knocked at the door of her lips as though to inquire if there were any god-daughters that could be had for the money. It was clear both to Mr. and Mrs. Chickenhackle that the answer would be strongly in the affirmative.

"That settles the matter! we decide upon Elizabeth Mary," said Mr. Chickenhackle.

CHAPTER IV.

BETWEEN TWO STOOLS.

DID Mr. Chickenhackle say that the matter was settled, and that they had decided that the name of

Elizabeth Mary should be given to the sole daughter
of his house and heart? That gentleman was never
more deceived. The matter was anything but settled ;
as he speedily found to his sorrow. Instead of having
cut the Gordian knot, he had but further complicated
its difficulties.

Miss Meagrim had no sooner left his house, than
she went to make a call—a most friendly call, of
course—on Miss Ricketts. What took place at that
important interview between these Rival Queens of
Spinsterhood, can only be inferred from the expressions
let fall by Roxana Ricketts, when she called (an hour
afterwards) upon her brother John, and attacked him
with the information she had received from Statira
Meagrim.

Poor Mr. Chickenhackle was bewildered.

" Do not suppose, brother John," said Miss
Ricketts, her maiden's breast all aglow with fiery
indignation,—" Do not suppose that I, who am your
sister, am to be made of second-rate importance to a—
a person—yes, a person," continued Miss Ricketts, as
though that word was the most opprobrious epithet in
the dictionary, " who is no relation at all to you, like
I am, brother John ; but only an aunt of Mrs. C.'s ;
and, thank goodness, that is only a connection, and
that relationship does not go by the wife's side. I am

surprised at you, brother John, for not standing up for the rights of your own family, but allowing them to sink in the balance, when weighed against the pretensions of that person !" Miss Ricketts tossed off this opprobrious epithet, hissing hot from the coals of her wrath, with as much complaisance as though it were a steak, and she the cook.

" Why, my dear Mary !" said Mr. Chickenhackle, who, as he only *deared* his sister in times of perplexity, was evidently now reduced to that state ; " what can it possibly matter whether the child is called Elizabeth Mary, or Mary Elizabeth ? "

" Then," rejoined Miss Ricketts, with much sternness and decision of manner, as though she would thereby repress all remonstrance and wavering, "if it does not matter, let the child be called Mary Elizabeth."

Mr. Chickenhackle scratched his head so violently, as to impress the spectator with the idea of fleas.

" If she is called Mary Elizabeth, I am content, brother John, " said Miss Ricketts.

" Why, you see, my dear Mary," replied brother John deferentially, not to say abjectly, " Miss Meagrim is rather what you call crotchety, and she particularly wishes that *her* Christian name should come first."

" I am equally what you call crotchety, brother

John, and I particularly wish that *my* Christian name
should come first ;" said Miss Ricketts, like an indig-
nant Echo."

"But, how **is** it possible for both names to come
first ? it's a moral impossibility, you know !" And
again, Mr. Chickenhackle would **have** impressed the
spectator with **the idea of fleas.**

"I have nothing to do with impossibilities, brother
John," said Miss Ricketts, sententiously and enigmatically ; "all I have to do is with possibilities ; and
there is every possibility, that, if I find myself made
of inferior importance to that person," (which opprobrious epithet she again tossed off with a steak-like
hiss,) "by having *my* Christian name made to come
after that **person's** Christian name,—and if your
child, — my niece, brother John, and not my
great-niece, you will please **to** remember—if that
child is named Elizabeth Mary, instead of Mary Elizabeth, she will receive from me only a mere godmother's
present, as a silver mug, or something of that sort,—
instead of a legacy that will be more worthy of her
acceptance."

"Almost Miss Meagrim's very words !" groaned
Mr. Chickenhackle, in great perplexity.

"**And** the amount of the legacy she named, was—"
asked Miss Ricketts, as a feeler.

" Ten thousand was the figure," said brother John.

" I will make it **twelve**," said Miss Ricketts.

" You are very good, I'm sure," said brother John ; though he would have again impressed the spectator with the idea **of fleas.**

" Twelve thousand **pounds are not to be** thrown away for a trifle, brother John," pursued Miss Ricketts.

" They are not, sister."

" And it **is a larger amount than** ten thousand, brother John."

" There is **no denying it, sister."**

" Then, **if you wish your little daughter to inherit** this larger sum, **there is but one way by which you can** effect it."

" And that is——? "

" By calling her Mary Elizabeth ; making the Mary to come before the Elizabeth ; **as I** should have thought I came before that person in importance, brother John."

" Of course you do, **my** dear sister."

" Very well, **then ! you can now prove it to be so.** Name your child Mary Elizabeth, **and I** will give her twelve thousand pounds. Otherwise, not one penny !" And Miss Ricketts, having given her fiat, made her exit, cooking up some observation as she did so, in which the opprobrious epithet person spluttered with a steak-like hiss.

And again Mr. Chickenhackle would have impressed the spectator with the idea of fleas.

CHAPTER V.

A DOMESTIC DIFFERENCE.

" Why, my dear ! " cried Mrs. Chickenhackle, as her spouse entered her room ; " how rough your hair is ! Whatever have you been doing to it? you look quite wild."

" And enough to make me.   Here's Elizabeth Meagrim comes one minute, and says that if her godchild isn't christened with *her* name first, she shan't have *her* legacy; and then, the next minute, comes Mary Ricketts, and says that if the child isn't christened with *her* name first, she shan't have *her* legacy ! And how can it be done ? We can't make the two names march side by side, like school-girls out for a walk. I'll declare there's more fuss about it than it is worth."

" What *it !*" rejoined Mrs. Chickenhackle.   " Surely by *it* you do not refer to your child, Mr. C. ?"

" Bless me, Maria, no !" answered the Mr. C., some-what testily. "No, poor little thing ! and certainly it seems but right—quite a parental duty, I may say—that we should endeavour, if possible, to secure *both* legacies for her ; not so much for the sake of the money itself, but that it will place her above the frowns of the world, if anything should happen to us, and if I should not be quite as successful in business as I hope to be."

It is astonishing what ready excuses people can make for filthy lucre's sake !

"Then, has Miss Ricketts also promised her a legacy ?" asked Mrs. Chickenhackle.

"Twelve thousand, on the condition she is called Mary Elizabeth, *versus* Miss Meagrim's ten thousand on the condition she is called Elizabeth Mary," replied her husband.

Mrs. C.—I am afraid, John, that we must offend one of the godmothers.

Mr. C.—I am afraid so, Maria.

Mrs. C.—And there cannot be the least doubt which.

Mr. C.—Not the ghost of one, my dear.

Mrs. C.—Then we are agreed that the chief god-mother shall be my aunt Meagrim ?

Mr. C.—Your aunt Meagrim ! No ! My sister Ricketts.

Mrs. C.—No, John ! that will never do.

I

Mr. C.—But it must do, Maria. My sister bequeaths more than your aunt does.

Mrs. C.—But then, dear John, you know that I too have expectations from aunt Meagrim, and that she has it in her power to do more for us than, perhaps, Miss Ricketts can, or will ever do.

Mr. C.—But, Maria! Miss Ricketts is my sister.

Mrs. C.—I am aware of that, John. So, she should act as a sister, and give up the point when asked to do so.

Mr. C.—Nonsense, my dear! she should do nothing of the sort. As my sister, she has the first claim.

Mrs. C.—You need not talk about nonsense, my love. I am sure that aunt Meagrim *has* done, and *can* do, more for us than Miss Ricketts *has* ever done, or *can* ever do.

Mr. C.—You do not confine yourself to the truth, my darling. My sister's property is double your aunt's any day of the week.

Mrs. C.—You need not rub all the hair off your head, Mr. C. I am sure it is going quite fast enough, and that you have not so much that you can afford to lose any.

Mr. C.—I shall do just as I please with my own property, Mrs. C., and so will my sister with hers. I will not have her insulted before my very face.

Mrs. C.—I was not insulting her. It was you that were insulting my aunt, Mr. C.

Mr. C.—Your aunt may be shot, Mrs. C.

Mrs. C.—I see how it is, Mr. C.; you wish to quarrel with me, and you seize the very moment when I am worn down with weakness to do so—a time, Mr. C., when most men, who call themselves men, would think more of their wives, and their poor helpless little babes. (*Begins to turn on her entire system of water-works.*)

Mrs. C.—Now pray don't, Mrs. C. For goodness sake, don't! you know how I dislike crying. Pray compose yourself, Maria! I didn't intend to hurt your feelings, my dear; I didn't, upon my honour! It's only this absurd fix into which these two old maids have pushed us that has worried me. Let them both go to Jericho, and their names with them! and we'll call baby by your name—or my name—or any-one's name—Tom, Dick, or Harry, for the matter of that—so as to get us out of this difficulty. There, let's think no more about them; but get other godmothers, if they won't stand unless they are tied to their stakes. Ha, ha!

But Mr. Chickenbackle's joke did not have the effect of composing his wife's mind. She—good and cautious mother—naturally did not wish to throw aside the chance of securing at least one legacy to her daughter, while she did her best to keep in her aunt's "good books," and to secure for herself that place in Miss Meagrim's will, to which she had for some years hopefully and trustfully looked.   So, she turned to the unconscious source of all these difficulties, who was peacefully slumbering in the crib at her side, and addressing it in a highly-injured tone, said, "My poor little baby! your cruel father wants to rob you of ten thousand pounds!" and, with that, her entire system of waterworks were again brought into play.

This was putting quite a new aspect upon the matter; and Mr. Chickenhackle felt rather uneasy at thus being presented in a guise of a pilferer of his own flesh and blood; his remonstrance, therefore, was tinged with some warmth of colouring.

"Now, hang it, Maria! what folly you talk! when I am working night and day to scrape up for that child. If it was possible, I should like to secure both the legacies for her; but, as it is not, why, in the name of all that's reasonable, let us have the larger. And, as Miss Ricketts bids the higher figure, why, let us choose her for godmother number one; and let baby's name be Mary Elizabeth."

But Mrs. Chickenhackle said—I suppose from the spirit of opposition—"I prefer that Miss Meagrim should be godmother number one—as you call it; and that baby's name should be Elizabeth Mary."

Mr. Chickenhackle testily rubbed his head, and strode out of the room; saying, as he got to the door, "Mary Elizabeth!"

"Elizabeth Mary!" called out his wife. And then as the door closed with a bang—like a goose as she was—she cried over her child as though she were ready to break her heart.

And thus were those two loving hearts, who had rarely had a word of cavil since their wedding-day, set at loggerheads, and plunged into difficulties of position as well as temper, and all about a child's name. Truly, after this, which of them could say that there was nothing in a name?

CHAPTER VI.

THE CUTTING OF THE GORDIAN KNOT.

ANOTHER week had passed. Mr. Chickenhackle had made a separate and final appeal to each of the maiden ladies, but without effect. They were not to be stirred one inch from their position.

"If my name does not come first, she shall lose the legacy!" said Miss Ricketts.

Said Miss Meagrim —" She shall lose the legacy, if
my name is to come second."

Mrs. Chickenhackle took part with her aunt.   Mr.
Chickenhackle decided in favour of his sister.   The
ass between two bundles of hay was not in a more
tantalising position than was little baby Chickenhackle,
placed between her two tempting legacies.   Was it
possible to secure both for her ? that was the question.
It was the subject of her father's waking thoughts,
and nightmare dreams.   The seven days' progress of
events had done nothing towards lessening the difficulty of the situation.   On the contrary, by the end
of the week, the subject had become even more in-
volved, and had assumed a fresh phase of complication.

"If your husband," said Miss Meagrim to her
niece, " persists in declining my legacy to your child,
he will also oblige me to leave my other property elsewhere than where I had intended to leave it."   And
she gave her niece one of her stiletto looks.

"If, brother John," said Miss Ricketts to Mr.
Chickenhackle, " you suffer your wife's choice to prevail, you will not only oblige me to omit your child's
legacy, but will also compel me to bequeath the rest of
my property otherwise than I had intended."   And
she looked at her brother with great meaning, but

with an expression that suggested the distillation of verjuice — if any one had the hardihood to squeeze her.

So, here was a further complication! Mr. Chicken-hackle was fairly bewildered, and knew not what to do for the best. The honeymoon of baby's life was now upon the wane, and it was necessary that a day should shortly be fixed for the christening. The name given to the child would be the signal for war; and, of all wars, a domestic war is most to be dreaded, especially when, as in the present case, a heavy pecuniary loss would be entailed by the contest. The days passed on sadly and drearily. Mr. Chickenhackle went about with such a despairing look, that his business friends began to whisper that he must be in difficulties,— little guessing the real difficulties of his position. When he came to look at his baby, he would stand over her, and moodily shake his head, and sigh heavily; and then walk away with only such words as " Poor thing ! she little knows the troubles she has brought upon us." Then, the mamma would burst into tears ; at which display of her entire system of waterworks, her husband would testily stride out of the room. It was a miserable household : and all this, because their child must have a name.

But—and this " but," I warn you, gentle reader, is a very Malmsey butt, in which all these tears and

difficulties are to be drowned—but, on the morning of
the last day of baby's honeymoon of existence, Mr.
Chickenhackle, who had left the house early with the
aspect of a man who was about to rashly make away
with himself, suddenly appeared before his wife in a
highly excited state of joyousness.   He kissed her—
he kissed the baby—and it is probable, that he would
have kissed Mrs. Toosypegs herself, had not that
highly-valued monthly nurse just left the room in
order to prepare for her departure to her next patron.

"Whatever is the matter, John?" Mrs. Chickenhackle might well ask as an explanation of her husband's apparent lunacy.

"This is the matter, Maria.   I have found it out!
The problem is solved!   The knot is cut!   The riddle
is answered!   Baby has both legacies!   I have just
been to each of the godmothers, and they are perfectly
satisfied! and, bless my life, what owls we must have
been not to have thought of it before."

"Thought of what?"

"Why, MARELI to be sure!"

"Mareli! what's that?" asked Mrs. Chickenhackle,
not knowing whether it was an Indian pickle, or some
new soothing syrup for infants.

"Mareli!" rejoined Mr. Chickenhackle; "why,
baby's name, of course!"

"Baby's name! do try and explain yourself—if you

are able to do so, Mr. C.," said his wife, with unpleasant suspicions as to her husband's state of mind.

"Well! I'm not quite sure that I can do so, Maria: at least not very clearly; for, I've not yet recovered from the surprise of my discovery, and its successful results. This was how it was: I was on my way to sister Ricketts to see if she wouldn't relent, or do something to help us out of our fix, when it flashed across me in an·instant. By it, I mean 'Mareli.' Why—I thought—why not take the halves of those two old maids' names, and tack them together, as fish and flesh are joined to make a mermaid; then, the two names will go on an equality, ambling together side by side like a pair of carriage horses, and not trotting one before another like a man driving tandem. So, said I to myself, if I take the first three letters from each of the old ladies' names, and join them together, the thing is done; for, one name will be as prominent as the other, and so, it will make both come first, don't you see?"

"I think I begin to see what you mean, dear John."

"This is our position:—Miss Elizabeth Meagrim insists on *her* name being the prominent one; so does Miss Mary Ricketts. Very good; we'll accommodate

both parties.   Take the first three letters of Mary, **and**
the first three **of** Elizabeth, and make one word **of**
them.   There **it** is—MARELI: a name containing
quite as much of Miss Meagrim as it does of sister
Ricketts;—six of one, and half a dozen of the other;
—and, though I say it of my own invention, a very
pretty name too!"

"Well! I don't know about that, dear John; but,
if it answers the desired object, we could find beauty
in a less ugly name than Mareli.   But, are you quite
sure that it has settled the objections raised by the two
godmothers?"

"Quite!", replied Mr. Chickenhackle, gaily.   "I
went to each of them, charged with the electricity of
my own brilliant idea.   The shock of the communica-
tion was less severely felt than I had expected.   They
each appeared to be pleased that their godchild should
bear a new and **entirely** original name, to the creation
of which **their** own names **had** solely contributed; and
so, as there was no preference, there was no jealousy.
They were soon propitiated; and they amicably agreed
to stand to the little ducksy-wucksy by the name of
Mareli."   And Mr. Chickenhackle fell upon his baby
with an exaggerated display of parental affection.

"**And are the** legacies quite safe?" asked the pru-
dent **Maria.**

" Safe as the **Bank.** **To** make matters as smooth as I could, **I proposed to Miss Meagrim that there** should **be no** difference **in the amount** of the legacies ; and that I **would ask sister Ricketts to** reduce her legacy from twelve **thousand to ten.** But Miss Meagrim would not hear **a word of this, and** declared that **she** would raise **her legacy from** ten thousand to twelve. So, there, **my dear Maria, you see** the worth of my invention—not including what it will secure to you and me, **personally.** Mareli is a twenty-four thousand **pounder!"**

It **was even as Mr. Chickenhackle** stated. The rival queens had **ceased** their **rivalry.** Statira and Roxana had shaken hands **with** greater fervency than **they had** ever performed that accustomed action, and, as they **drew nigh to** (what even they were obliged to confess) their old age, they grew wiser, and became better friends. Their little god-daughter, who had once been **a cause** of difference, now became a centre of union : and this **was not** the least charm wrought by MARELI.

SYRINGALINE.

TABLES were laid at the " Grange," tables with plenty
    upon them :

There were they laid on the grass, out of doors, in the
    cool of the evening ;

Guests swarm'd around them like bees, though sweeter
    by far than the honey

Were the smiles on the lips of the ladies, all laughing
    in glee and good-humour.

Toxophilites all were the guests, and had come from an
    archery meeting,

Where, all the day in the sun, they had riddled the
    targets with arrows,

And got in the gold in a way that fabulous Tell didn't
    dream of.

As the giver of all the good cheer, so Mrs. Bright
    headed the table :

The kindest was she of the kind, the generous and the
    good-hearted,

The fountain of mirth and good-humour diffusing its
sparkles around her.

And there at the table she sat, like a motherly hen
with her chickens !

And there was her cousin, Ka teHerbert, dispensing
the tea and the coffee ;

Kate Herbert the happy and blooming, Kate Herbert
the calm and contented,

Smiling serenely on all, with lips quite distracting to
look at,

Like a bright sunbeam condensed and endued with
health and vitality ;

Roses and lilies combined to make up the bloom of her
features ;

White were her shoulders and neck, white as the
Parian marble ;

White were her arms, too, and hands—white and refreshing to gaze on—

As she sat at the end of the table, looking as cool as a
cucumber !

Long they sat over their tea, and loud was their mirth
and their laughter ;

And well, too, they plied the provisions,—the fowl
and the ham, and the veal-cake,—

And diminish'd the goodly supplies that the " Grange "
ever seem'd to o'erflow with.

Then, having satisfied hunger, sharpen'd by archery
    practice,
Rose they from tea in a body, and went round the
    beautiful gardens,—
The gardens that circle the house, as the rich-spangled
    robe does the monarch,—
And soon the book-muslins and flounces had spread
    themselves over the green turf.
Red rose the full-moon upon them, and nightingales
    sang in the bushes,
Rich was the scent of the flowers, and the night-breeze
    was laden with odours ;
All was delicious and sweet as they walk'd in the cool
    of the evening.
Then they divided for play, as happy as children and
    careless ;
And half were to hide in the shrubs, and half were to
    seek for the hidden,
And curious concealments were found, and rare hiding-
    places selected ;
And great was the searching and hunt after some of
    the party assembled ;
But greater the joy and the mirth when at length they
    were found in some corner,
And laughingly dragg'd from their haunt, betray'd by
    their dress and their giggling.

Then for a change they had "Tick," and swiftly they
    fled round the flower-knots,

Winding adroitly about, like a hare when pursued by
    the greyhounds :

The gentlemen shouted and roar'd; scream'd, squeal'd,
    and cried out the ladies ;

A Babel of unruly tongues made pleasant with musical
    laughter ;

So that passers-by out in the road stopp'd in wonder
    and made the inquiry,

" What on earth means this riot and noise, and what
    is the cause of this kick-up ?

Is it a mad-house asylum, with the lunatics out for an
    airing,

Or the famed Agapemone House, with the inmates all
    playing at hockey ?"

Thus the travellers, wondering, ask'd—so great was the
    noise of the madcaps.

Then when heated and fagged were the girls, and all out
    of curl were their ringlets,

They paused for a moment in play, and debated what
    next should their game be ;

When a bright thought Blanche Howard illumed, and
    she cried, her face beaming with pleasure—

" Oh ! come, and I'll teach you 'Tirza,'—a game I've
    seen play'd up in Yorkshire !"

So she set them all out, two and two, a gentleman each
    with a lady,
Standing all round in a ring, each the waist of the
    other embracing.
And she show'd how the game must be play'd, and
    laughingly taught them the lesson ;
And the scholars soon willingly learnt the task of their
    beautiful mistress.
Long play'd they all at the game, and mirthfully chased
    one another,
And the red moon looked silently down on their glee
    and their innocent pleasure.
So then they all waited awhile, and some went in-doors
    for the music,
And others stroll'd gently about, and listened outside
    to the singing.

But where is Kate Herbert the while, and what has
    Kate Herbert been doing ?
She has wander'd away with " her beau," the pleasing
    and talented Henry :
Down, 'mid the shrubberies' maze, were the walks are
    retired and winding ;
Down, 'mid the shrubberies' maze, where the walks are
    so lonely and narrow :

Away from the gaze of the rest, away from the jeers
    of the scoffers;

There they go gently along, and each is entranced by
    the other.

Conversational powers are his, and the theme of his
    converse is fruitful :

In ecstacy blissful she lists, while her bright eyes are
    sparkling with rapture,

And the little loves fan the young flame as they lurk
    in the roses around them.

When they emerge from the walk—" Oh ! where have
    you been ? " is the question.

Then answered Kate Herbert, at once—Kate Herbert
    the calm and contented,—

" To see the Syringa we went, and to gather its beau-
    tiful blossoms."

Then doubtings were muttered around, and the name
    was suggested of Walker;

And one, with a prominent nose, said, " Miss Howard,
    wilt thou pray do likewise ? "

So she laugh'd, and she would not at first; but her
    love of botanical knowledge

Induced her at last to consent, and they started to see
    the Syringa.

Then he of the nose led her down where Kate Herbert
    had rambled before them;

And Blanche shook her forest of curls, and laughed out
    as though she enjoy'd it;

And the moon lighted up her soft cheeks and contour
    of her classical profile,

And lovely and beaming she look'd, and bright as the
    flowers around her,—

Diffusing a sunshine around, as she moved in the light
    of her beauty.

Then he of the nose led her on, and they rambled away
    from the others;

And backwards and forwards they went, and searched
    for the famous Syringa:

All round the gardens they went,—down 'mid the
    shrubberies' windings,—

Hither and thither and round,—by the hothouses and
    by the stables,—

Diving about in the shrubs, and exploring their inmost
    recesses;

And the red moon was lighting them on in their search
    for the famous Syringa.

Ever anon, from the shrubs, as they wander'd now
    hither and thither,

There was heard a peculiar sound—peculiar and yet
    not uncommon—

A light gentle smack, followed close by a volley of
    musical laughter,

Musical laughter that rose, and was caught up by mu-
    sical echoes,

Till it fell on the ear of the Night, and awakened the
    Dreamer to raptures.

Then giggled the ladies, and said, "Lo! Blanche now
    has found the Syringa :"

And then, when they met her, they asked, "Pray what
    is it like,—this Syringa ?"

Then answer made he of the nose : "I know what it's
    like, and I'll tell you.

Its blossom is full, rich, and sweet, and wondrously
    like to the Two-lip ;

In loneliest places it thrives, but requires some forcing
    and 'Oh'ing :

Warmth, too, enhances the bloom, and the moon
    brings it out to perfection :

And happy is he who can find, but happier he who
    may pluck it,

For it brings its possessor such joy, that straightway
    he falls into raptures,

And long will he dwell o'er its sweets, the fragrant
    delights of its blossom,

Till his soul is o'erflowing with bliss, and his mind,
    too, with happy contentment ;

So great are the powers and charms of this wonderful,
    famous Syringa."

Then the ladies all choruss'd and said, " Truly won-
    derful is this Syringa !"

And one to Blanche Howard observed, as she archly
    look'd over her shoulder,

" To judge from your dishevell'd hair, greater power
    still has this Syringa :

For first when you went on your search, your ringlets
    were seemly to look at,

And now they are all out of curl, and looped up in
    negligent *bandeaux :*"

And further she would have run on, but Blanche
    Howard had run off with laughter,

And ere she had time to say more, they were speedily
    summon'd to supper.

In they all pour'd like a stream—like an impetuous
    river ;

Down at the tables they sat, the tables all groaning
    with good cheer,

And violent hands were soon laid upon delicate dishes
    and dainties.

There by her Henry ensconced, pleasant and blissful
    to look at,
There was Kate Herbert herself, Kate Herbert the
    calm and contented,
Looking quite cool and refreshed with the sight of the
    famous Syringa.
And so look'd Blanche Howard herself, as she sat
    there just over the table,
With her hair smoothly drawn back in bands from her
    white intellectual forehead,
Showing off to advantage her face, and her regular
    classical features.
Happy and mirthful was she, and he of the nose sat
    beside her,
Minister'd e'er to her wants, and plied her with
    chicken and lobster,
Constantly gave her Champagne, and with her divided
    the *bon-bon*,
And, like a wise man, ne'er forgot his own wants and
    peculiar likings.
Happy and pleasant was she, and buoyant as ever in
    spirits,

And every fair guest seem'd to catch the contagion of
    mirth and of laughter,

And stale jokes were laughed at as new; dim wit
    shone as brightly as better;

And loud was the laugh at the pun, though poor was
    its aspect and meaning,

For where all are ready for mirth, they require but
    little incentive,

But will readily echo the laugh, though they know
    not the cause of the laughter.

Thus the supper pass'd gaily away, and the midnight
    pass'd into the morning,

And the night was refreshing and cool, and the grass
    was with no dew upon it,

So they set out of doors once again, and all went to
    see the Syringa,

And all were enraptured and charm'd—all who had
    found out its fragrance.

And then the gay music struck up, and lithesome feet
    tripp'd to the Polka,

And couples spun briskly about, and twirl'd, too, and
    flew in the *deux Temps,*

Then sat out of doors to get cool, and made merry
    parties among them.

So the evening ended at length, as all things sublunary
    must do;

And all went away to their homes, away from the
    scenes of their pleasures,

Talking away as they went o'er the many delights of
    the party,

Still feeling joyous with glee, untired, unflagging in
    spirits;

And the red moon look'd down on them all driving off
    happily homewards.

L'ENVOY.

I bid ye good-night and adieu! ye maidens so glee-
    some and comely:

Ye have gladden'd the path of my life with brief
    moments of unalloy'd pleasure;

Ye have brought me a sunshine awhile with your
    smiles and your musical laughter;

And now your bright presence is gone, and—I'm in a
    cab—with my sister!

Farewell, happy maidens, farewell! Good-night, now
    our pleasure is over:

May care never wrinkle the brow that now is so smooth
    and so placid,

Or dim the rich lustre of eyes that now are so brightly
    resplendent;

On their thrones ever lightly as now, may the lords of
    your bosom be seated ;*

May you peacefully slumber in rest, with good angels
    watching around you,

And may dreams bring you back all the bliss you re-
    ceived from the famous Syringa.

---

* " My bosom's lord sits lightly on his throne."—*Romeo and Juliet.*

POTTED KNOWLEDGE.

The royal road to learning has been well nigh gained. The age that has brought travelling to such a degree of perfection that a man can now be conveyed from one end of the kingdom to the other with no greater discomfort to himself than if he were passing the hours in his own study—this age of rapidly getting over the ground in the smoothest and easiest way (accidents excepted) has also been remarkable for the production of a class of literature whose "mission" (to use one of the slang terms of the day) is to enable the reader to get over a good deal of literary ground in the most expeditious and agreeable manner. To change our metaphor—the genius of Cookery has been brought to bear upon literature, and has resulted in the production of Potted Knowledge. Such a result was absolutely necessary to meet the hasty requirements of this rush-about business age. The merchant and tradesman who would be foremost in the race for success is

K

compelled to be so great a martyr to his business that
he has not even time for his martyr's steak, but is
forced to content himself with a simpler noon-day
meal, which must be devoured hastily, savagely, and
mechanically, like the fitful refreshment-room dinners
of travellers by an express train.   To this class of
eaters enforced hastiness is not a matter of choice, but
of necessity; and it has, therefore, been an important
subject of inquiry with all those who have any care
for that portion of their anatomy which was wont to
be called the stomach, but which the periphrasis of
this mock-modest age delicately denotes as " the diges-
tion,"—it has become a matter for earnest inquiry
with these people of digestions liable to be disordered,
whether or no their food could not be so prepared that
it should afford the maximum of nourishment in the
minimum of space, and be devoured with such swift-
ness and ease that its consumption should offer little
or no interruption to business, at the same time that it
discharged all its looked-for functions.

Now, it has generally been conceded, that the object
of which these digestive inquirers were in search was
to be found in the shape of potted meats.   In them
was to be discovered the maximum of nourishment in
the minimum of space, and such a rejection of useless
material, and condensation of all that was nutritious

and valuable, that an ox (or all that was worth eating of him) might be squeezed into the compass of an oyster-barrel, and a calf could be crammed into a quart-pot. What cooks have done for meat, the purveyors of mental food have effected for literature, and Potted Knowledge is now prepared and sold to meet the demands of an age in which high-pressure is called into requisition for all the needs of our outward life and inward sustenance.

Although the process of manufacture is tedious, and requires considerable judgment and skill in the selection of the component parts, yet, when judiciously treated, the article may be made not only palatable but nutritious. The recipe is exceedingly simple. As soon as it has been determined what form the Potted Knowledge shall take—whether history, science, art, politics, geography, travels, &c.,—the ingredients are ordered from the nearest public libraries, the choice pieces are cut out and minced, the scraps are boiled down, the residuum is compressed into as small and light a compass as possible, and the result is Potted Knowledge. When it is ready for use it may be labelled after this fashion: " Analysis of Art," " Abbreviated Anecdotes," " Abstracts of Accounts," " Brief Account of Birds and Beasts," " Condensed Histories of Cockchafers," " Concise Notes on Churning," " Compendium of Chess," "Handy-book of Husbandry," "Index to Literature," "Literary Laconics," "Manual of Mushrooms," "*Résumé* of Reports," "Succinct Notes on Schools," "Summary of Something and Everything," "Synopsis of Sports," or any other names, in short, which would convey the idea of a work so comprehensive as to contain in a brief space the condensed information of encyclopædias, dictionaries, gazetteers, and a hundred books of reference.

Potted Knowledge, too, assumes another form than that in which it is seen bound up in calf, cloth, or morocco. For example, our quarterly reviews, scientific journals and reports, and the monthly and weekly literary periodicals, supply a very goodly amount of Potted Knowledge. The diligent reader of these various reviews can form a very fair idea of the literature, politics, science, and art of the day; and without the expense of subscribing to Mudie's, Hookham's, Bull's, or Booth's, and without giving himself the trouble to read the produce of their libraries and to form an opinion as to the merits or demerits of the works, he can prattle about the books of the month to his fair neighbour at the dinner-table or dance, as though he had really devoured their multifarious contents. In an hour's desultory reading he will have imbibed the condensed literature of the past month, and have been put in possession of sufficient material for evenings of booky small-talk. For this he has to thank many a skilful *chef* and *cuisinier*, whose natural gifts, improved by cultivation and industry, have come between him and his idleness or overwork, and have administered to him those meals of Potted Knowledge, which, like the forcemeat pellets to the turkey poults, have brought him up to the requisite standard of literary fulness.

Swift evidently had the idea of Potted Knowledge in his mind, when he compared the labours of an author to chickens which required months to fatten, but were eaten in a few minutes. It is a just comparison. The reader quickly consumes the fare that the author places before him, although the author may have been months or years in its preparation and cookery. But, with that large class of persons, who, from lack of time or trouble, derive their knowledge of the chief literature of the day mainly through the aid of reviews, the author's chickens must be subjected to a condensation of cookery before they can be made acceptable to their peculiar palates. And this is the office that falls to the lot of the reviewer. The critic, in a certain sense, stands between the author and a large class of desultory readers, who are either of too busy, placid, or bovine a nature to peruse for themselves works of which their position in society may demand some knowledge, and on which they may be socially required to pass judgment. The task that they are either unfitted, unwilling, or unable to do for themselves, the critic does for them. The author fattens his chickens for the literary market, and the critic steps forward as the *chef de cuisine,* and cooks up the chicken into a *salmi,* or boils it down into chicken-broth, or in some other suitable method prepares the Potted Knowledge for the reader.

First comes the author, who gives us the essence of the works of all previous writers; and then comes the critic who condenses the work of the author, and presents the very pith and marrow of it to the reader. The author has to work months and years; the critic has to labour hours and days; and the final result is Potted Knowledge, which may be devoured in a few minutes. In the instances where this condensed information is given through the medium of Reviews, much, of course, must depend upon the artistic nature of the critic's cookery. If he be a critic, like the one in Sydney Smith's joke, who never read a book before reviewing it for fear of being prejudiced, then his critical cookery of the work cannot be of that Potted Knowledge character which will convey to the reader the very spirit and essence of the book; but rather will it partake somewhat of the nature of haggis, of

which it has been said that it is " fine, confused eating ;" for, the critic will necessarily be driven to gene-
ralities, and the work which is professedly reviewed
will be merely a peg on which to hang the reviewer's
exercitations. But, if he be a real and true critic,
with a full sense of his calling and responsibilities, he
will carefully consider the author's chicken in its ever
aspect, and, simply garnished by his own judgment,
he will endeavour to set before his reader its very pith
and essence in the shape of Potted Knowledge.

THE HEART'S MISGIVINGS.

LINES ON THE PICTURE BY FRANK STONE.

" Some glory in their birth, some in their skill,
   Some in their wealth, some in their body's force,
Some in their garments, though new-fangled ill,
   Some in their hawks and hounds, some in their horse

.   .   .   .   .   .

" Thy love is better than high birth to me,
   Richer than wealth, prouder than garment's cost,
Of more delight than hawks and horses be,
   And naming thee, of all men's pride I boast:
Wretched in this alone, that thou may'st take
   All this away, and me most wretched make."

Shakspeare's Sonnets.

THERE'S a languor in the air,
   And a stillness all around,
The landscape wide and fair
   Is in dreamy silence drown'd ;
The sky is blue and bright,
   And all is fair to see ;
But the maiden sigheth sadly,
   " Ah ! he careth not for me ! "

The royal sun goes down
   Like a bridegroom to his bower,
Flash from his golden crown
   Bright beams on tree and tower;
But that scene of summer splendour,
   Though so beautiful to see,
She heeds not, but sighs sadly,
   " Ah ! he careth not for me !"

Like as snow her forehead white,
   Dark her hair as raven's wing,
Bright her eyes as stars of light,
   Sweet her lips as flowers of spring ;
Quick her breathing heaves her bosom,
   Like the throbbings of the sea,
And she sighs again more sadly,
   " Ah ! he careth not for me !"

Against the old stone wall
   She leans with clasped hands;
Nought to her that castled hall,
   Nought to her those wide-spread lands ;
For on the youth that's near her
   She gazes fixedly ;
But she sighs, and thinketh sadly,
   " Ah ! he careth not for me !"

He sits, while *she* doth stand,—
  He laughs, *her* eyes grow dim,
He sees that only on his hand,
  She sees but only him :—
A hawk is on his hand,
  And a dog is at his knee,
And the maiden sigheth sadly,
  " Ah ! he careth not for me !"

" No ! he careth not for me,
  Though my heart is all his own ;
Since I saw him ne'er 'twas free,
  And 'tis his, and his alone !
'Tis no slight thing or unstable,
  'Tis no trifle that I've given ;
For my *life* to him I've trusted,
  And he is now my heaven.

" Pure as that sky above,
  With not a cloud to dim,
Is the pure and holy love
  That I have shrined in him ;
But he laughs whene'er I tell him
  That like this my love can be."
And once more she sighed sadly,
  " Ah ! he careth not for me !"

" Oh ! he little thinks the anguish
    His unconcern can bring,
  Or deems the heart can languish
    In life's first early spring ;
  But thinks that merry girlhood
    Must *ever* thoughtless be."
  And again she sighed sadly,
    " Ah ! he careth not for me !

" When he speaks mine eyes do glisten,
    And I feel a burning glow
  Come o'er me as I listen
    To the voice so well I know.
  When he comes I know his footstep,
    And I thrill with ecstacy !
  But "—she paused, and sighed sadly,
    " He careth not for me !

" No ! his hound, his steed, his bird,
    To him are dearer far,
  And no reproachful word
    Shall his youthful pleasures mar.
  Yes ! these, my heart's misgivings,
    Shall not damp his happy glee."—
  But the maiden sigh'd more sadly,
    " Ah ! *would* he'd care for me ! "

Down went the royal sun,
  And the purple twilight came,
And the stars rose one by one,
  Still the maiden gazed the same !
But unmoved by twilight hour,
  That " hour of love," was he,
And the maiden sighed sadly,
  " Ah ! he careth not for me ! "

There's a languor in the air,
  All around's in dreamy rest,
And love is everywhere
  Save in *his* youthful breast ;
More entranced with his hawk
  Than that maiden fair is he ;
And her heart's misgiving is,
  " Ah ! he careth not for me ! "

ACROSTIC CHARADES.

"Lysander riddles very prettily !"

Midsummer Night's Dream, Act ii., Sc. 3.

CHRISTMAS, more than any other season, is the very time when the wide-spread families of Riddles, Conundrums, Enigmas, and Charades love most to meet their friends.

For then even the oldest and weakest may be fearlessly brought forward, with the full confidence that they will be greeted with the respect due to the many years during which they have been bandied to and fro in the world, and in which—notwithstanding that they may have met with repeated failures—yet (paradoxical as it may appear) they have invariably been found to have answered. And then, too, even the poorest and most threadbare—those who, in pantomimes and burlesques, may have been brought from one stage to another, and have even been reduced to beg a laugh at a circus—even these miserable ones are not driven away in their tatters, but, when introduced to the Christmas guests, are received with that spirit of good-will which is the very soul of the Christmas season, and with that indulgent kindness which is undoubtedly the largesse that we should bestow upon them in return for their endeavours to win our smiles, and to provide us with harmless amusement.

In how many homes will this kind of innocent recreation be indulged in when the time of merry Christmas has again come round! It will find its place in quiet family circles, where the little children gather together at their games—in the old English farm-houses, where the ruddy fire lights up a century of comforts; as well as in stately mansions, where in the

> "Tudor-chimneyed bulk
> Of mellow brickwork,"

there is an ancient hall, with a real yule-log blazing on the spacious hearth, and around it a goodly gathering of men and maids. There, perhaps, when that particular time of the evening shall have come, as it came

> "At Francis Allen's on the Christmas-eve,"

and is told by Tennyson with such unctuous brevity—that time when

> "The game of forfeits done, the girls all kiss'd
> Beneath the sacred busb,"

the assembled company may, over their wassail-bowl,
start a conversation similar to that which passed between Mr. Francis Allen, "the Parson Holmes, the
poet Everard Hall," and Mr. Tennyson himself, who
(as he tells us)

> . . . . . . "held a talk,
> How all the old honour had from Christmas gone,
> Or gone, or dwindled down to some odd games,
> In some odd nooks like this :"

and having, perhaps, *acted* a charade at some earlier
part of the evening, they may now, as they sit there
chatting round the fire, and unable to bestow upon
Christmas those olden "honours" so deplored by the
quartet of epic-loving friends at Francis Allen's, these
modern Christmas-keeping men and maids may possibly fall back upon "odd games," even to the *asking*
of riddles and charades. In which sport, we trust
that we may be permitted to join them, bringing, as
our portion of the entertainment, a few Acrostic Charades.

These novel and ingenious riddles have lately been
introduced, and afford much amusement. Their introduction here will, we think, be acceptable to our
readers, many of whom may desire to exercise their
invention in the composition or solution of these
agreeable novelties. To the young, especially, they
may be made the vehicles of much instruction, and

to all they may afford harmless and rational amusement.

They are composed in this way. Two or more words are selected, independent of each other as to verbal connection, and yet having some dependence on each other as regards their allusions and signification. This connection may be that between a general and his victory (as Wellington, Waterloo; Horatio Nelson, the Battle of the Nile); an author and his work (Charles Dickens, Little Dorrit); a potentate and his palace (Napoleon, Tuileries; the Lord Mayor, Mansion House); an inventor and his invention (James Watt, the Steam Engine); a spot and its celebrity (Fotheringay Castle, Mary Queen of Scots; the Lakes, Wordsworth); or any other similarly legitimate connection, provided that the word or words, chosen on either side, contain the same number of letters. This is necessary for the sake of the acrostics.

There are two acrostics formed by the selected pair of words. Thus, in the words above quoted, if we take "The Lord Mayor, Mansion House" (which are the only pair of those words that contain the same number of letters), we can put either "The Lord Mayor," or "Mansion House" to form the first acrostic. If we put the former, then the first letter on the one side is T, and the first letter on the other

side is M. We must then look out for some word
that begins with T and ends with M, selecting only
such words as are substantives or proper names. Suppose we take "Term:" we must then mention it, in a
charade form, in one line of prose or verse (if more
than one line is used it must be so stated), as, for example, "In college and court I bring work to all,"
referring to the term-time of Universities and Inns of
Court. The next letters for the next line will be H
and A; and we must select a word commencing with
H and ending with A, as Hermia (of the "Midsummer Night's Dream"), of whom we might say—"In
love with my next word Lysander did fall." Then we
come to E and N, and so on, all through the twelve
letters of "The Lord Mayor" and "Mansion House."
When we have got through these twelves lines we
shall have formed our two acrostics; and it must be
denoted (by a break, or by writing "The Words,")
that we have come to the end of our acrostics, in
order that the guesser may know the number of the
letters—the number of the words he must find out
how he can. We must then add a few more lines, in
order to explain the whole—of course taking care to
describe "The Lord Mayor" and "Mansion House"
as enigmatically as possible. But, as example is
better than precept, we will here give a specimen of

the Acrostic Charade, with its answer, and an explanation of that answer. If, however, we should have
been fortunate enough to make the foregoing explanation sufficiently lucid to the reader, he can, if he so
pleases (being thus warned beforehand) avoid looking
at the answer; and, not allowing his eyes to wander
beyond the last line of the charade, puzzle out its
meaning for his own amusement. With this note of
warning we will begin; premising that each line of
the introduction contains the signification of a word,
and that the lines are perfectly independent of each
other.

THE LETTERS.

(1.) I can take vengeance without taking ease;

(2.) Without saying why, I on industry seize.

(3.) I am the name by which Paris was known;

(4.) I am an organ that up am oft blown.

(5.) I, as an exile, advance on the scene,

(6.) With great Alexander's most beautiful Queen.

(7.) I'm the pastoral poem Theocritus penn'd;

(8.) And I'm Cleopatra's last-welcom'd friend.

(9.) I am her Majesty, put into Latin;

(10.) And I wear a coat that is smoother than satin.

(11.) I am the man who first weather'd the Cape,

(12.) I'm architectural as to my shape;

(13.) And I brought a fate which men cannot escape.

THE WORDS.

The century's wonder—a raree-show
　　Design'd from a leaf out of Nature's book.
If you guess my two words, you then will know
　　How the one from the other existence took.

In the lines descriptive of "The Letters," we have endeavoured to give the various ways in which the Acrostic may be expressed. The first word has to begin with **V,** and end with **C**; there are few words of this kind, except adjectives, such as *viatic, vivific, vitriolic,* &c., which should be regarded as inadmissible, being words of slight importance. In a case like this a *ruse* is perfectly allowable for the purposes of the Acrostic; and we, therefore, took the word "Vengeance," without taking its *e*'s, by which means the word would end with *c,* and thus give us the word required. In like manner, in the second line, we seized on "Industry," without saying *y*—the elision of the final letter, making the word begin with *I* and end with *r,* which was what we required. In the third line the guesser is intended to be driven from the scent by another kind of *ruse,* for the "Paris" here referred to is not the city of Paris, but the *Paris* of "Romeo and Juliet," and the name by which he was known was "the County Paris," and "County" is the word we require. The answer to line No. 4 is "Times"—an influential "organ" that is alternately lauded and condemned (*vulgariter*, "blown up"), according to the opinions or temper of the speaker. The exile of No. 5 is the "Outcast." No. 6 is "Roxana," the beautiful captive and Queen of Alexander the Great. No. 7 is "Idyl," the name given to the pastoral compositions of Theocritus. No. 8 is the "Asp,"—"as sweet as balm, as soft as air"—that sucked brave Cleopatra's life. No. 9 is "Regina," the Latin name of the "Queen." No. 10 is the "Eel," with his slippery skin. No. 11 is "Gama," the Vasco di Gama, who has the reputation (now destroyed by Mr. Timbs, in his "Things Not Generally Known") of having "first weathered the Cape." No. 12 is "Ionic," one of the orders of architecture; and No. 13 is the "Apple," through which Death was introduced. And now, if you put together, in their regular sequence, the first and last letters of these words, they will form into the required words of the answer—VICTORIA REGIA, CRYSTAL PALACE.

Now that we have shown the *modus operandi* of constructing, and solving, the Acrostic Charade, we will leave the subject for the amusement of our readers, merely subjoining, for their practice in the art, a few brief specimens.

NO I.—THE LETTERS.—(6.)

Untax'd I brighten the poor man's home—
  My wings wave over the beauty's brow—
I steal by St. Petersburg's gilded dome—
  While Bomba's subjects before me bow.
A cook had reason to dread my name,
Though I carry the tidings of pride and shame.

THE WORDS.

A mighty centre of woe and wealth;
  A world in little, a kingdom in small.
A tainted scenter, and foe to health;
  A quiet way for a wooden wall.
Find out these words as soon as you can, sir;
And then you'll have found this acrostic's answer.

NO. II.—THE LETTERS.—(5.)

I brighten even the darkest scene—
I very nearly an ostrich had been—
I with a hood once pass'd all my days—
I am a fop in the play of all plays—
To its greatness the city of Bath I did raise.

THE WORDS.

I'm a mark of judgment, of taste, and wit,
  O'er a crowd of pages I rule the roast;

I mix with choice spirits, while choicer ones sit
Around, while I give them full many a toast.
Of my two words, my first is squeez'd into my second,
Although at its head it is commonly reckon'd.

NO. III.—THE LETTERS.—(8.)

The wisest warrior earth can name,
A well-won fight, well known to fame;
The source of wealth to Boniface,
The muse of love and lyric grace;
A Russian town where sailors stop,
What parting friends will vow to drop;
A wondrous tale of jealous fears—
The hidden cause of actors' tears.

THE WORDS.

Two mighty words in the page of history,
   The one was won and the other was lost;
Though we find it again, by a kind of mystery,
   To the topmost summit of power tost.

NO. IV.—THE LETTERS.—(15.)

The Chinese sailor dreads my fearful ire:
For, beauty was my death—I slew my sire:
And I no beauty ever had to lose:
And so I weigh men down with heavy dues:

The earth has often felt me a great bore :
To highest flights of tragedy I soar :
For me, the batsman cheerfully goes in :
Me, from inclosure, grateful cockneys win :
An orchestra I am, without a ray :
And from my six you must take ten away :
My empire's built on rags, and not on swords :
The faith I taught, the wildest words affords :
In a thin silk I hide myself from sight :
I gain'd a world-wide name in Indian fight :
And, when I'm ended, then's "put out the light."

THE WORDS.

With shatter'd limb and fever'd brain,
    The soldier on his pallet lay ;
And never thought to see again
    His home and friends—far, far away :
And ne'er to reach that cot in Devon,
    Where he had pray'd to end his life ;
And never more—unless in Heaven—
    To look upon his child and wife.
And, while he lay so weak with pain,
    With dry lips parch'd, and all athirst,
With swimming sight, and fever'd brain,
    My Second cheer'd him in my First.

Like some bright angel of a dream,
   She came and stood beside his bed;
And stayed his bark, as, on the stream
   Of Death, it floated towards the dead.
She changed his couch from pain to rest,
   With loving word and tender hand;
She soothed the sorrows of his breast,
   And brought him from the shadowy land.
And when he saw his home again,
   He into joyous rapture burst,
And bless'd the blissful moment when
   He saw my Second in my First.

NO. V.—THE LETTERS.—(14.)

The cricket merrily proclaims my name;
The brethren three who fought for Roman Fame;
Me, as their home, the needy poets make;
When I'm ahead, the stoutest hearts will quake;
The monster that sets up John 'gainst Thomas;
Eusebius when he was taken from us;
The man who wont believe unless he sees;
When I am dead I sweetly rest in peas;
Mid fiends and goblins I now take my place:
The sculptor loves me for my clear white face;

Unto the castle's stronghold now I glance :
And now I spy a beauteous queen of France ;
At winter's misty threshold I remain ;
A pair that part to quickly meet again.

THE WORDS.

Master of tears and laughter ! High arch-priest
   Of the great mysteries of this Life's fane !
Great Wizard of the North, South, West, and East,
   When shall we look upon thy like again ?

We will not wreathe your head with bays,
   To be a laughing stock for all the gapers ;
But, when to thee a monument we raise,
   Around your hair we'll curl your own fam'd Papers.

ANSWERS.

"Oho ! I know the riddle !"—*King Lear*, Act v. Sc. 1.

Number I. The LETTERS are *Light, Ostrich, Neva, Despotism, Owhyhee, News :* and the WORDS are *London, Thames,* the latter odoriferous river, and common sewer of Great Britain's metropolis, being " the silent highway " for the wooden walls of Old England.

Number II. The LETTERS are *Lamp, Emu* (the

L

"tail-less ostrich"), *Marian* ("Maid Marian," the companion of Robin Hood), *Osric* (the courtier "water-fly" of *Hamlet*), and "Beau" *Nash*. The WORDS are *Lemon, Punch*. Mr. Mark Lemon (the "*mark* of judgment," &c.), be it remembered, is the editor of *Punch*. It has been remarked that, curiously enough, three lemons entered into the composition of *Punch ;* namely, Mark Lemon, Leman Rede, and Laman Blanchard.

Number III. The LETTERS are *Wellington, Alma, Tap, Erato, Revel, Line, Othello, Onion*. The WORDS are *Waterloo* and *Napoleon*.

Number IV. The LETTERS are *Simoom, Cenci, Ugliness, Taxes, Artesian, Ristori, Inning, Hampstead Heath, Orchest-ra, si-X, Pen, Irving, Taffeta, Aliwal, Life*. The WORDS are *Scutari Hospital*, and *Miss Nightingale*, words that will ever rise together in a Briton's thoughts with the deepest feelings of gratitude and respect to England. "Santa Filomena!"

Number V. The LETTERS are *Chirp, Horatii, Attic, Rock, Law, Eusebi-us, Sceptic, Duck, Imp, Carrara, Keep, Eugenie, November, Scissors*. The WORDS are *Charles Dickens,* and the *Pickwick Papers*.

"Around his hair we'll curl his own famed Papers."

THE OLD WINDOW-SEAT.

THERE are spots by Love made blessed,
   And hallow'd by its spells ;
There are scenes where Memory lingers ;
   There are haunts where Fancy dwells ;
But the green and shady bowers,
   And the grove where lovers meet,
Recall not happier hours
   Than that dear old window-seat.

Ye may love the fields and meadows
   Where as children ye have play'd,
The lane arch'd o'er with hawthorn
   Where your first love-vows were made ;
Your scenes of happy childhood
   May be fraught with fancies sweet ;
Ye may love the fields and wild wood,
   But I—that window-seat.

I have been where gold and jewels
    Flash'd in the beauty's hair ;
I have listen'd to the whispers
    Of many a lady fair;
But not those scenes of splendour,
    Or those hours so bright and fleet,
Can waken thoughts so tender,
    As that dear old window-seat.

Would you ask me why I love it ?
    A thousand answers find
Their utterance in the memories
    They swiftly bring to mind :—
There I saw her, there I woo'd her,
    There betrothed we first did meet,
And my first love-kiss was stolen
    On that dear old window-seat.

There, in the tender twilight,
    On the summer evenings long,
To a low and plaintive air she'd sing
    Some old familiar song ;
And her bright eyes brighter glisten'd
    As she sang with voice so sweet,
While I sat entranced, and listen'd,
    On that dear old window-seat,

There we sat, aye many an hour,
   Though but minutes seem'd they then ;
Blissful moments such as they were
   I shall never know again !
There, our day-dreams fondly tracing,
   We have pass'd the hours so fleet,
And sat in love embracing,
   On that dear old window-seat.

It was upon a May-day,
   As we sat there side by side,
That with trembling hope I ask'd her
   To be my bonny bride.
With cheeks and bosom glowing,
   She heard then my entreat,
And "yes" she softly falter'd
   On that dear old window-seat.

But a sudden change came o'er her,
   And she weaker grew each day,
And we knew the young and beautiful
   Was passing fast away.
She long'd that on her cheeks again
   Should breathe the zephyrs sweet ;
So we bore her where she wish'd us,
   To that dear old window-seat.

The twilight deepen'd round us ;
  She saw the red sun set,
" I die ! " she feebly whisper'd,
  " Oh ! do not me forget."
We watch'd the death-glaze dim her eye,
  Feebler her pulse did beat,
And, murmuring my name, she did die
  By that dear old window-seat.

MOONRISE.

ALL calm and silently the moon doth rise!
   Like some reproving spirit, sad and pale,
Bending o'er sinful earth, with watchful eyes
   Marking men's deeds, and all their woeful tale
Of shame and crime, and dread enormities.
   All pale she looks; the stars come twinkling out;
White fleecy clouds float lightly o'er the skies.
   The earth lies hush'd, save when the children's
       shout
Tells that the tired cottar's reach'd his home;
Humble it is, but many a palace dome
   Has seen less happy faces, less delight,
Than greet *his* coming. Sound is heard no more;
The sleepy wave scarce ripples to the oar;
   And e'en the clock tells drowsily the hours of
       night.

THE STORM-SPIRITS.

THE Spirits of the Storm are out to-night,
  Like mighty millions mass'd in banded battle;
    And, through the crystal courts and coral caves,
    Deep down beneath the billowy boiling waves,
  Their clattering coursers' hurried hoofs do rattle.
Rushing and raging in their foaming might,
They toss unto the storm their manes of white,
  And bear their spirit-riders up on high—
    With shining foreheads in the lightning gleam-
        ing—
  To meet the tempest raining from the sky.
Then, down they plunge into the yawning deep,
  Laden with spoil of some rich argosy,
While, on their billowy pillows, brave men sleep
    That sleep of death which knows no rise or
        dreaming.

CARRIAGE - AND - FOUR GHOSTS.

WHAT is the use of one's being a ghost, and driving a ghostly carriage-and-four, unless one's ghostly magnificence and state is to be made known to the world? If I am to be made a carriage-and-four ghost of, I should at any rate desire for my friends to be made aware of the fact. Without their cognizance, it would be no pleasure to me to be rattled along by my " posters of the sky and air."

Actuated by this feeling, I now desire to repair the omission made by Mrs. Crowe, the ghost chronicler and seer, and to do justice to those carriage-and-four ghosts, whom she has not thought fit to embody in her spirited narrative. Tardy justice to these neg-lected spectres is better than none ; and my humble efforts may do somewhat in rescuing them and their stately carriages from oblivion.

It seems, then, according to.the superstitious belief of a great mass of people, that certain persons who have misconducted themselves while inheriting their fleshly tenement, are condemned to revisit the glimpses of the moon, and, as perturbed spirits, to find no rest; but it also appears, that a select few of these spectres, instead of being " doomed for a certain term to *walk* the night," like the ghost of Hamlet's father, and the vulgar herd of spectres, are accommodated with carriages, and *ride* through the night at the heels of four horses. Thus, there are even ghosts that can keep their carriages, and their carriage company; and can be independent, moreover, of all taxes and turn-pikes. It frequently happens that the horses which draw these ghostly carriages are headless; as is the case with the carriage-and-four ghost at Caistor Castle, the seat of the Fastolfes; and also with the ghost of the Devonshire clergyman, who rides in a carriage drawn by four headless horses up the lane to the church in which he had been accustomed to do duty. Tales of gentleman ghosts who travel in a similar state, are told in connection with the mansion of Parsloes, Essex; and Hardwicke and Haddon Halls, Derbyshire. None of these are mentioned by Mrs. Crowe; and it would appear that she had never heard of the Haddon Hall carriage-and-four ghost, for she says, "I never heard of a ghost being seen or heard in Haddon Hall, the most ghostly of houses."*

The spectre of the Devonshire clergyman appears to have been unpopular; for the tale goes, that twelve parsons were procured to "lay" the ghost, but failed in their attempt, through one of their number befriending the spirit and telling him their plan of action. His ghostship, therefore, "knawed the trick," as the relators of the anecdote express it, and refused to be laid. The villagers of Cumnor say that they were more fortunate with the ghost of poor Amy Robsart, —which was laid by three-times-three Oxford parsons. It would be curious to know the ceremonies made use of on these occasions.

I have said, that the four horses which drew the carriage of the Devonshire clergyman were headless horses. Carriage-and-four ghosts appear to have preferred steeds of this description: probably because they give a more unnatural air to the *cortège.* To carry out the headless principle to the uttermost, the horses were occasionally driven by headless coachmen, and even the occupants of the carriages dispensed with their heads, in order that their coachmen and steeds might not be put out of countenance. But ghosts are

* "The Night Side of Nature," chap. xiii.

not the only kind of people who sometimes lose their
heads.   A carriage-and-four, with headless horses and
coachman, is driven about between Bury St. Edmunds
and Great Barton.   The occupants of the carriage are
a headless gentleman and lady.   Like the late Mr.
Mytton, they drive across the country "as the crow
flies," scorning the road, and going over hedges and
ditches with all Mr. Mytton's *sang-froid*, until they
arrive at their destination in "Phillis' Hole," in the
parish of Rougham.   Another carriage-and-four ghost
of this description favours with his presence the
village of Acton, in Suffolk.   He travels in unusual
state, being accompanied by headless grooms and out-
riders.   The park gates fly open at his approach, and
he is whirled on to a place called "the Nursery Corner,"
—a place where some great battle took place in old
Roman times.   At the Roman station of Caistor,
too, where Sir John Fastolfe built a castle, the people
believe that yearly, at midnight, a dark coach, drawn
by headless horses, drives into the courtyard, and
carries away some unearthly passengers.

   The spectre of Sir Thomas Boleyn, (the father of
Anne Boleyn, Queen of Henry the Fat,) is another
carriage-and-four ghost, but one who deserves a para-
graph all to himself, for he takes his rides in a singularly unique manner.   He is not content with his

headless coachman and horses, nor is he satisfied with simply detatching his head from his shoulders, but he revisits society, carrying his head under his arm, as though he were St. Denis himself, and as though his head was a crush *gibus* hat, which he puts under his arm for convenience' sake. As regards this head, however, thereby hangs a tale. As it lies snugly under his arm, flames of fire issue from its mouth, and the spectator is horror-stricken at the sight. Sir Thomas resided at Blickling, near Norwich ; and he is condemned to travel thus, with his flaming head underneath his arm, in his carriage drawn by four headless horses, and driven by a headless coachman, for the term of one thousand years. Alas, poor ghost ! Indeed, Sir Thomas is altogether an out-of-the-way ghost, and has to take a longer drive than the ordinary carriage-and-four ghosts ; for twelve bridges, in the vicinity of his former home, have to be passed over by him, ere he can find rest for another twelvemonth. It is but "only once a year" that he takes his ride, but that once is quite enough to last him for the twelve-month. I wonder what carriage-duty he pays. Perhaps he has compounded !

The flames of fire that issue from Sir Thomas's mouth, are imitated (gross plagiarism !) by nearly all the carriage-and-four ghosts who drive teams with their full complement of heads. When the horses carry their own heads, they generally snort fire: sulphurous flames of a most unearthly character are emitted from their nostrils. Lady Lightfoot's steeds are of this description. Her Ladyship was kept a prisoner in the Court-house at Little Shelsley, Worcestershire, and was afterwards foully murdered there. At night, she comes in her ghostly, fiery carriage-and-four, and drives round the rooms where she was imprisoned and murdered; of course, these chambers are unoccupied, so she has them all to herself; and, as she is whirled through the rooms, her piercing screams ring through the house (if any one is awake to hear them). Then she drives out of doors, and dashes into the moat; the water seethes and bubbles, and the carriage and fiery horses disappear.

Another carriage-and-four ghost haunts the West of Norfolk. On the anniversary of the death of the gentleman whose spectre he is supposed to be, his ghostship drives up to his old family mansion. The gateway is walled up; but what does that signify? He drives through the wall—carriage, and horses, and all —and is not seen again for a twelvemonth. He leaves, however, the traces of his visit behind him; for, in the morning, the stones of the wall through which he had driven over-night, are found to be loosened and fallen; and, though the wall is constantly repaired, yet the stones are as constantly loosened.

Another carriage-and-four ghost haunts Leigh, a picturesque village between Worcester and Malvern. This ghost is familiarly called "Old Coles." In the days of his flesh, he tenanted Leigh Court; but, being soon encumbered with debts, " which," as Mr. Habingdon says in his account of him, " like a snow-ball from Malvern hill gathered increase," he was obliged to sell his family estate to Sir Walter Devereux. So, according to the retributive justice of superstitious belief, his restless spirit is now made to revisit the scene of his former dissipation. With his four carriage-horses snorting sulphurous flames, he is dragged on at headlong speed over hedge, and ditch, and banks, and trees, and finally, over Leigh Court itself, until his drive is ended by the waters of the Teme, into which his fiery coursers plunge with a plashing hiss.

I was once told, by a College friend, of a carriage-and-four ghost that haunted his father's house, in the county of Wexford, Ireland. This ghost went by the name of " The Brigadier ;" but I have now forgotten whether any reason was given for the visit of this spirit. I am not aware, too, if the spectral carriage was reported to have been *seen*; but, that it was *heard*, and that distinctly, I had the assurance of my friend,

who told me that they had frequently heard the sound
of the wheels rattle past the windows up the carriage-
drive, and then the sound, as of the sudden pulling-
up of the carriage when it had reached the hall-door;
and that servants, new to the house, had been so
deceived by the sound, that they had rung the stable-
bell to order round the grooms to the carriage, and
had themselves gone to the door to receive the expected
guests.

Chavenage Hall, in the Cotswold Hills, is singularly
honoured, having a coach-and-*six* ghost and a Royal
coachman. The legend springs out of the times of the
Great Rebellion, when the then Lord of the Manor,
suffering the arguments of Ireton and of a Puritani-
cally inclined brother, urged through the whole of a
livelong night, to prevail against his own better conscience and the prayers of a saintly sister, consented to
come to town and give his vote for the murder of his
King. The ill-advised man had not only been super-
naturally warned beforehand, but his sister, in a moment
of inspiration, had prophesied the extinction of the male
branch of his family if he gave his vote as Ireton
desired. From a deathbed embittered by the pangs of
remorse, and on which he sought to make some amends
by a public acknowledgment of his fault, his parting
spirit was conveyed in a Royal coach-and-six, driven

by the headless spectre of his injured Sovereign. It seems a deal of trouble for that excellent monarch to have taken about a comparatively insignificant country gentleman, but, of course, his Majesty knows his own affairs best; and as the honour is repeated every time a Lord of Chavenage dies at the Manor House, no doubt there are special reasons we are not acquainted with.

Another carriage-and-*six* ghost is supposed to haunt the city of Edinburgh. Hard by the Castle, in a house in the West Bow, once lived a Major Weir, a person so eccentric and mysterious that his very cane was thought to be invested with miraculous powers, and to be able to go out shopping! A sister managed the Major's domestic affairs, and he himself was fond of attending religious meetings, where he discoursed with great fluency. At length, he was struck down with sickness, and fearing to die, sent for the magistrates, and confessed to them that he and his sister had been guilty of many horrible crimes. The sister attested to the truth of this confession, and she and her brother were executed. Their house in the West Bow was deserted, but nevertheless its windows would be lighted up at night with ghostly candles, and sounds of revelry would be heard within, until a spectral coach-and-six, with headless black steeds, would dash up from the Lawn-market, and after receiving the Major and his sister, would drive away again. The house, therefore, remained untenanted for half a century, when it was taken by a man named William Patullo. But on the first night of his occupancy, a headless beast came to the bed where he and his wife were sleeping, and so alarmed them, that they left the house and never entered it again. And another fifty years elapsed before another tenant could be found for this house of bad repute.

THE WANTON SUNBEAM.

I CAME upon her quickly! she was sitting
　Upon a bank embrownëd in the shade;
All round about the sunbeams bright were flitting,
　But did not dare to come where *she* was laid.
And, like to gleaming guards about a portal,
　Who watch, and yet to enter are afraid,—
So they, as angels bright around a mortal,
　Did keep around and guard this lovely maid.
But one bright sunbeam pierced that twilight bower,
　And thrust aside the leaves that made the shade;
And, softly as the zephyrs touch a flower,
　He slid into her arms and o'er her bosom stray'd;
And, wanton, kiss'd her cheeks, her lips, her hair—
"O Jove!" I cried, "that I that sunbeam were!"

SPRING-TIDE.

APRIL lay blushing in the lap of May,
   And so, mid smiles and tears, told all her love;
   The sunshine was around them; and above,
The clear blue sea of heaven tranquil lay.

The buds were out on ev'ry springing flow'r;
   The leaves were thick on ev'ry bursting tree;
   The viewless larks were gushing forth their glee,
And Eden odours stole from ev'ry bower.

The velvet turf was daisied o'er like snow;
   Their yellow bells the cowslips did disclose,
   To ring the requiem of the last primrose,
That pale beside its brooklet dear did grow.

The butterflies to their loved flowers had gone;
   The fern was springing in the wild deer's path;
   And modestly, in her sequester'd bath,
The nymph-like* water-lily's white limbs shone.

        * " Nymphæa alba."

The garden trees were creaming o'er with bloom,
   The wild wood-cherry and the plum, the same ;
   In purple dress the meadow-orchis came,
In golden robes the king-cups and the broom.

A pleasant murmur stole the woodland through ;
   The singing birds a merry music made ;
   And where the lime-trees threw a soft green shade,
The belted bees their tiny trumpets blew.

The silver streams that flow'd the meads among,
   With a light laughter went upon their way ;
   The lambs, with their ewe-mothers fond, did play,
And nightingales pour'd out their souls in song.

And everything was full of light and love,
   And fresh'ning green and bloom were everywhere ;
   Nature seem'd bursting into flow'ry prayer,
Unto her beauty's Source enthroned above.

SIDDONIANA.

BYRON was accustomed to say, that of actors Cooke
was the most natural, Kemble the most supernatural,
and Kean the medium between the two; but that
Mrs. Siddons was worth them all put together. He
also records that he never saw Miss O'Neil, because
he had made a determination that he would not see
any one who was likely to disturb his recollections of
Mrs. Siddons, whose

> " Thrilling art
> O'erwhelm'd the gentlest, storm'd the sternest heart." *

As I believe that every *new* scrap of information
concerning this gifted woman will, however scanty and
puerile, possess a fictitious interest, attributable to
the charm of its subject, I shall here note down some
memorabilia relative to Mrs. Siddons, which have not
hitherto appeared in print, and which may prove ser-
viceable to the biographer, and amusing to the general
reader.

* Byron's Address at the Opening of Drury Lane Theatre,
October 10, 1812.

Those most unsatisfactory and miscalled " Memoirs of Mrs. Siddons," by Boaden—which (outdoing the proportions in Falstaff's pottle of sack), for one page of information regarding Mrs. Siddons, give us some three or four score relative to her contemporaries, and to foreign matters—tell us that, " in her youthful acquirements she had probably few aids beyond those of her parents." Her other biographers do not appear to have hazarded information on this point, and pass over her girlhood in a few sentences. Now, as regards her " youthful acquirements," I have been fully assured that she went as day-scholar to private schools of some note, both in Worcester and Wolver-hampton, the theatres * at which places were under her

---

* At this time, there was no regular "theatre" (building) in Worcester. The companies of comedians who visited the place gave representations at "the Great Room, at the King's Head, in High Street;" or at "the Trinity Hall;" or at "the Theatre, near the Town Hall." The present theatre in Angel Street was erected in 1780, by Mr. James Augustus Whiteley (the then manager of the theatre at the King's Head), with the assistance of twelve subscribers. The first notice of theatricals at Worcester occurs in the "Worcester Postman," for January 4, 1717, where is advertised that, "for the Benefit of Mr. *Butcher*, jun., and his Wife," would be acted, "at the King's Head, in High Street, *that celebrated* Play *called* ŒDIPUS, King of THEBES, *with several New and Diverting Entertainments between the Acts particularly a Pleasant Scene between a Drunken Man and his Wife, in a Tavern.* Beginning exactly at six o'clock. VIVAT REX ! " In 1784, we find advertised at the new theatre, among other startling attractions, " *Harlequin's Vagaries;* in which Harlequin will escape down his own

father's management. It is very evident that the acquirements of " the Siddons" were of a far different order to those of "the Fotheringay;" and it is but reasonable to suppose that Miss Kemble had the advantages of a school education in all or most of those towns in which her parents made any lengthened stay. The school to which she went in Worcester was Thorneloe House School, then kept by a Mrs. Harris—no myth, but a veritable and kind lady, who, fascinated by the beauty and talents of the little Miss Kemble, would not accept of any *honorarium* for her tuition. A lady who has lately died in Worcester, in her hundredth year, was at Thorneloe House School at the same time with Miss Kemble, and well remembered her. At first, Miss Kemble was somewhat looked down upon by her schoolfellows, as being " a player's" daughter; but at length came the occasion of her triumph, and rise in popularity. The girls got up

throat! and fly across the stage from balcony to balcony." In the next year we have dancing dogs; and Mr. Mappler takes his benefit, who, "in the course of the evening, will take a *brief lick* at his own head." (Whatever may this have been?) In 1788, "the very moral pantomime of 'Don Juan'" is performed, for the benefit of Mr. John Palmer, when, "N.B. The Ladies are respectfully informed that the fire in the last scene will not injure the finest cambric handkerchief." In 1795, the Chevalier D'Eon takes a benefit " at the age of 68, cutting her bread with a sword." In 1805, Master Betty is engaged to play for eight nights at a thousand guineas, but consents to receive a less sum.

some amateur theatricals, in which Miss Kemble's stage knowledge and **talents** brought her prominently forward, as manager and chief performer, and secured for her not only the admiration, but also the friendship of her school companions. On one of these occasions she **had** to personate **a lady dressed in a loose** kind of gown known **as a sack (or** *sacque*); and, as the proper materials wherewith to manufacture it were not forthcoming, the future Mrs. Siddons displayed her inventive and **constructive powers, by fashioning the** required garment out of **some sheets of blue sugar-paper.**

Miss Kemble **had made her** *debût* upon the boards at a very **tender age.** When her infantile appearance excited **the** disapprobation of her Bœotian audience, who hooted and hissed **her, her** mother led her forward, and made her repeat the fable of **the** " Boys and the **Frog."** She **did this with** such ability and *point*, that even the rustic critics **could not** but help seeing that what might be fun to the **boys might prove death to the** poor little frog; **so they abstained from hissing, and** ever afterwards received **their little frog with a** kindly welcome. **Miss Kemble's first** appearance on **the** Worcester stage appears **to have taken place when she** was in her twelfth year. In 1767, her father became the manager of the Worcester Theatre, which was then held " at the Great Room, at the King's Head, in High

M

Street," where Mr. Ward (the father of Mrs. Kemble, and the restorer of Shakspeare's monument) had been manager. At this time the managers of country theatres were driven to various ingenious expedients, in order to evade those penalties upon unlicensed playhouses threatened by the Act of 1737. This Act—which first established a dramatic censorship in this country—was introduced by Sir Robert Walpole, in consequence of a seditious and abusive farce, called the "Golden Rump," that had been offered to the managers of the London theatres; but its effects are now mitigated by the Act of the 28th of George III., which empowers magistrates, at general or quarter sessions, to license theatres in the country for the performance of dramatic entertainments. The common practice, in order to evade the penalties of this Act, was, to advertise and *charge* for a concert, and, between its parts, give the plays and farces *gratis*. I shall by and by quote a very singular evasion of the Act, from a play-bill issued by Kemble in Wolverhampton.

Mr. Macaulay's practice of looking through files of old newspapers for various points of information on minor, but yet important matters, can be advantageously imitated in the matter of theatrical biography. Acting upon this idea, I have turned to the file of "Berrow's Worcester Journal" (a file that reaches back

to the early part of the eighteenth century), to see
what light it would throw upon Mrs. Siddons's early
days. The first advertisements of "Mr. Kemble's
Company of Comedians" is dated February 12, 1767.
He announces—"A Concert of Music, to begin
exactly at six o'clock;" and then follows the main
attraction of the bill of fare: "Between the parts of
the concert will be presented, *gratis,* a celebrated
historical play (*never performed here*), called CHARLES
THE FIRST; the characters to be dressed in antient
habits, according to the fashion of those times." The
play was chiefly performed by the members of the
Kemble family; for, among the *dramatis personæ*, we
find—"James, Duke of Richmond, *Mr. Siddons;*
Fairfax, *Mr. Kemble;* James, Duke of York, *Master
J. Kemble;* the Duke of Gloucester, *Miss F. Kemble;*
the part of the Young Princess, by *Miss Kemble;* and
Lady Fairfax, by *Mrs. Kemble.*"—"Between the acts,
singing by *Mrs. Fowler* and *Miss Kemble.*" So that
here we have the future Mrs. Siddons acting and singing at Worcester before she was twelve years of age.
Her musical abilities were of the highest order, and
she must, despite her youthful years, have been a valuable member of her father's company. Her brother
John was at this time in his tenth year; and, if he
and the other characters of the play were really dressed

"according to the fashion of those times," the pic-
turesqueness of the attire may have thus early imbued
his mind with that perception of its general fitness for
a conventional costume for the group of Shakspeare's
historical plays, which he retained to the last, and by
the carrying out of which—though at the expense of
antiquarian correctness and truth—he achieved a most
beneficial reform in stage costume.　The play of
" Charles the First " was no doubt an attractive one to
the inhabitants of " the Faithful City," and was repeated on February 14.

Two months after this, Miss Kemble's acting and
singing were again in demand, for the character of
Ariel in the " Tempest."　This, as I should suppose,
though it has escaped the notice of her biographers,
was the *first* of her Shakspearian delineations—the
rising of that brilliant Shakspearian star that culmi-
nated in Lady Macbeth.　On this account, therefore,
and also because the play-bill is in itself note-worthy,
I will here transcribe the greater part of it, mention-
ing such only of the *dramatis personæ* as were represented by the members of the Kemble family :—

" *Worcester, April* 16*th,* 1767.
" Mr. Kemble's Company of Comedians.
" At the Theatre at the King's Head, on Monday evening next,
　being the 20th of April instant, will be performed a Concert
　of Musick, to begin at exactly half-an-hour after six o'clock.

Tickets to be had at the usual places. Between the parts of the Concert will be presented, *gratis*, a celebrated Comedy, call'd

The Tempest; or, the Inchanted Island.

(*As Altered from Shakspeare by Mr.* **Dryden** *and* **Sir W.**
D'Avenant.)

With all the Scenery, Machinery, Musick, Monsters, and other
Decorations proper to the piece, entirely new.

Alonzo (Duke of Mantua), **Mr.** Kemble ;

Hyppolito (a Youth **who never saw a Woman**), *Mr.* Siddons ;

Stephano (Master **of** the Duke's Ship), *Mr.* Kemble ;

Amphitrite, by *Mrs.* Kemble ;

Ariel (the Chief Spirit), by *Miss* Kemble ;

And *Milcha*, by Miss F. Kemble.

" The Performance will open with a Representation of a Tempestuous Sea (in perpetual agitation) and Storm, in which the Usurper's Ship is Wreck'd ; the Wreck ends with a Beautiful Shower of Fire.— And the whole to conclude with a Calm Sea, on which appears Neptune, Poetick God of the Ocean, and his Royal Consort Amphitrite, in a Chariot drawn by Seahorses, accompanied with Mermaids, Tritons, &c."

Not the least curious part of this bill is its announcement of the "monsters and *other decorations*" (?), and the wreck, ending "with a beautiful shower of fire." Nevertheless, in this fashion was the " Tempest " produced by Mr. Kemble, twenty-two years after this, at Drury Lane, on the evening of October 13, 1789.

Perhaps Miss Kemble was permitted to make the best use of the gratuitous schooling that she received at Worcester ; for, although Mr. Roger Kemble's company remained there till July, and on July 9 (1797), performed "a dramatick opera, called 'King Arthur; or, the British Worthy,' written by Mr. Dryden;" in which Mr. Siddons, together with Mr., Mrs., and Master Kemble appeared, yet I do not find any further mention, during this season, of "Miss Kemble."

Roger Kemble was, for some years, the manager of the theatre in Wolverhampton, where he and his family were greatly respected; and where, as in Worcester, the future Mrs. Siddons had the benefit of that school education which Boaden and her other biographers have denied to her. A lady, to whom I shall afterwards allude, who enjoyed the friendship of Mrs. Siddons, was proud to talk of the days when she and the great actress were schoolfellows together in Wolverhampton. Kemble, of course, adopted the usual expedients to advertise his company; but one, at least, of his playbills is worthy of quotation, on account of the originality of the *ruse* by which the gratuitous exhibition was to be *paid for*. I cannot, unfortunately, give the date to this play-bill; but I should imagine it to have been issued in 1770. I shall mention only such of the *dramatis personæ* as belong to the Kemble family.

" MR. KEMBLE,

With humble submission, to the Ladies and Gentlemen of Wolverhampton, and the Town in general, proposes entertaining them on *Wednesday* evening, the 8th instant, at the TOWN HALL, with a

CONCERT of Vocal and Instrumental Musick,

Divided into Three Parts.

Between the several parts of the Concert (for the amusement of THE TOWN, and the further improvement of POLITE LITERATURE), will be continued

THE HISTRIONIC ACADEMY ;

With specimens of the various MODES OF ELOCUTION ; by INHABITANTS OF THE TOWN (for their diversion), without fee,

gain, hire, or reward.

The specimens of this night's amusement will be taken from a

COMIC OPERA, called

LOVE IN A VILLAGE.

Sir William Meadows, by MR. K—MB—LE ;

Young Meadows, by MR. S—DD—S ;

Rosetta, by MISS K—MB—LE ;

Housemaid, by MISS F. K—MB—LE ;

Madge, by MRS. KEMBLE.

And concluded with Comic Orations, &c., from

THE FIDLER turn'd CITIZEN.

„ This is to assure the Public that no Money will be taken for Admittance, nor will any Tickets be sold ; therefore, all persons inclined to attend the Concert are desired to call at Mr. LATHAM'S, at the Swan, where Tickets will be delivered GRATIS to his friends and acquaintance.

N.B.—Mr. LATHAM has a quantity of TOOTH-POWDER (from LONDON), which he intends selling in papers at 2s., 1s., or 6d. each. The same POWDERS may be likewise had at Mr. SMART'S, and Mr. SMITH'S Printing Office, and at the TALBOT, in King Street.

The Concert to begin at Five o'clock, and the Lectures exactly at half-past Six.

It is humbly hoped that no Ladies or Gentlemen will take it amiss, that they cannot possibly be admitted without a Ticket."

This is certainly very curious. The selling of the

tooth-powder, and the giving of the ticket, is like the old smuggling trick of selling a sham sack of corn, and making a present of the keg of brandy placed within it.

Soon after this, Miss Kemble was received into the family of Mr. Greatheed, of Guy's Cliff, near War- wick, in which romantic and hospitable home the two next years of her life were pleasantly employed. During the time that she was there, she does not appear to have been in any menial situation—(or, as one of her biographers phrases it, " in the *employment* of a lady named Greathead ")—but to have been treated as a companion, and as one of the family. There she practised the statuary art, and modelled busts that were long preserved by the family ; and there she continued to cultivate her love for theatrical matters, and, in the presence of Garrick, recited some speeches from " Jane Shore." Mr. Greatheed was himself a lover of everything connected with the stage, and a dabbler in theatrical composition. His play of " The Regent " was produced at Drury Lane Theatre in 1788, when Mrs. Siddons performed the part of its heroine *Dianora.* The play has long since passed into the limbo of dramatic pieces, and was not, at any time, calculated to assist in the ignition of the Thames ; but it was doubtless a proud moment for its

author, when his former *protégée,* attired as the heroine
of his piece, advanced upon the stage, and, with her ma-
jestic voice and thrilling periods, gave utterance to his
own composition.

But, though the atmosphere of Guy's Cliff was thus
charged, as it were, with the electric phenomena of the
stage, yet Miss Sarah Kemble would seem to have been
soon wearied of her retired life, and to have yearned
to once more tread those boards, which her ruling
passion had designated for her walk in life.   Accordingly, she left the hospitable home of the Greathceds ;
and at Trinity Church, Coventry, on the 26th of
November, in the year 1773 (the date and place are
not given by her biographers), being then in her nineteenth year, she became the world-renowned Mrs.
Siddons.

Mr. Siddons had been the leading member of her
father's company for some years past.   I have heard
that, before he took to the stage, he had been a barber
at Walsall, in Staffordshire.   He is described as being
" a fair and very handsome man, sedate and graceful
in his manners."   Although generally useful in a country theatre, he was but an inferior actor ; and Roger
Kemble was by no means pleased with his daughter's
selection.   I fancy that the young couple were privately
married, without the parental knowledge and sanction.

But, as what was done could not be undone, old Kemble sent for his daughter, and said to her, " Well, my child, I made you promise never to marry a performer, and you have not disobeyed me ; for the devil himself could not make an actor of your husband." By the way, this theatrical inferiority of the husband to the wife appears to have been the chief cause that led to their domestic disagreements and separation.

Let us glance at some of the doings of the Kemble family, during the two years that Miss Sarah was away from them at Guy's Cliff. On the evening of December 12, 1772, Roger Kemble produced at his theatre in Worcester "The Beggar's Opera, with the characters reversed ;" and twelve years later, on August 26, 1784, it was thus performed in London, for the benefit of the elder Bannister. Indeed, just about that time, the assumption of male characters by female performers was a plan usually resorted to when the theatrical bill of fare wanted a little spice of attractive novelty ; and a notable instance of this was brought forward at the Drury Lane Theatre in 1786, when the first part of " Henry the Fourth" was produced; on which occasion the part of Falstaff was *stuffed* (I suppose I must not say *filled*) by a *lady* (?)— a Mrs. Webb, who ought to have been (but was not) hooted for her pains. In 1773, we find Mrs. Kemble

performing the character of Ormisinda in " Alonzo,"
at her husband's theatre in Worcester, and in May of
the same year she appeared in " All's Well that Ends
Well." The theatre was then closed for a short time,
but was re-opened in June with " The Humours of
Parolles, and the Cowardly Captain ; the so-much-
esteemed comedy written by that excellent and inimit-
able poet Shakspeare "—in which the hero oppears as
Parolles (*alias* Tom Drum, the Cowardly Captain).
The other chief pieces performed at Worcester, at this
time, by Kemble's company were—" The Recruiting
Officer," " The Parthian Exile," and " Theodosius."
It was in this tragedy of " Theodosius " (as its hero)
that, three years later than this, on January 8, 1776,
the illustrious John Kemble first made his appearance
on the stage of Wolverhampton Theatre. He was
then in his twentieth year. Since, as a boy of ten,
he had acted at Worcester in the play of " King
Charles the First," and in the dramatic opera of
" King Arthur," he had received a sound and classical
education, first at Worcester, then at Sedgeley Park
School, near Wolverhampton, and finally at Douay.

Though we have seen that Mr. Kemble's theatre at
Worcester was opened for more than one short season
in the year 1773, yet that year was productive of much
discomfort to the poor players, whose existence the

chief magistrate of the city contrived to make a very chequered one. For, said Mr. Mayor, "neither player, puppy, or monkey" shall be suffered to remain in the city. For a time Othello's occupation was completely gone; but, after the Vigornian play-goers had been doomed to a few months of gloom, Mr. Mayor was compelled to relent before the storms of supplications and fires of epigrams with which he was on all sides assailed; and before the year 1773 had drawn to a close, the abstainers from theatrical sweets were treated to a very surfeiting of those dainties—the Faithful City being visited by no less than three companies of comedians in good time to assist in the Christmas revels.

We have already seen, that it was just at this time (November, 1773) that Miss Sarah Kemble left Guy's Cliff, and took unto herself a husband, in the person of one who had professed his affection for her, not only in private, but also—as Young Meadows, for example, in "Love in a Village"—on the public boards. One of the three companies of comedians who visited Worcester in December, 1773, was Mr. Kemble's; and they performed (on the 13th of December) "The West Indian," and "The Padlock." The characters of Charlotte Rusport in the former, and of Leonora

in the latter, were sustained by " Mrs. Siddons."
I imagine this to be the *first* occasion on which we
meet with that illustrious name which is now a household word, conjuring up before the mind's eye the
unequalled queen and muse of Tragedy.

Of her career from this time, we have pretty full
particulars; how she performed Belvidera at Cheltenham, and attracted the notice of the Hon. Mr. Boyle
and Lord Bruce; how this future Earl of Aylesbury
wrote to Garrick of their discovery of a rustic genius;
how Garrick thereupon sent down the Rev. H. Bate to
see and to report; how the reverend ambassador's
mission brought about Mrs. Siddons's *debût* at Drury
Lane Theatre, on Friday, 29th of December, 1775, in
" The Merchant of Venice, when the character of Portia
was performed by a Young Lady—her first appearance;" and how she failed to please the critics, and
was thereupon condemned to appear in minor characters, and in such pieces as " The Blackamoor Washed
White." All this we know, and her many town failures
and provincial ups and downs, before she reappeared in
all her glory on the London stage, on the 10th of
October, 1782, and made herself a name which, every
year, became more and more famous. Of these steps
and slips in her path to fame, her biographers have
given us a pretty full account; but there are even here

some few gaps which we are enabled to fill up with new material.

Gap the first is the birth of her first child. This occurred at Wolverhampton (where her father's company were then performing), on the 4th of October, 1774. The child was a boy, and was christened " Henry." It was not long after this—though the exact date I cannot give—that her success at Cheltenham, and her engagement at Drury Lane, caused her to take a " Farewell Benefit," and make a last appearance at Wolverhampton Theatre. On this occasion she delivered an address, *written by herself,* which is now printed for the first time. But one specimen of Mrs. Siddons's talents for versifying has hitherto been given to the public. This was her farewell address at Bath, in 1782, which commences with the following lines :—

> " Have I not raised some expectation here?
> Wrote by herself? What! authoress and player?
> True, we have heard her—thus I guess'd you'd say—
> With decency recite another's lay;
> But never heard, nor ever could we dream,
> Herself had sipp'd the Heliconian stream."

It appears, however, that she had endeavoured to do so at least once. The original manuscript of the following address was found among the papers of the late Miss Barney, of Wolverhampton, who was the schoolfellow and friend of the great actress :—

"[*Wrangling between* Mr. *and* Mrs. SIDDONS *heard behind the scenes.*]

Enter Mrs. SIDDONS.

Ladies and Gentlemen, my spouse and I
Have had a squabble, and I'll tell you why.
He said I must appear ; nay, vow'd 'twas right,
To give you thanks for favour shown to-night.
Said I—'Our thanks most certainly are due,
But that's a privilege sure belongs to you,
And well I know how sadly you would grieve
To lose one inch of your prerogative.'
He still insisted ; and, to win consent,
Strove to o'ercome me with a compliment ;
Told me, that I the favourite here had reign'd,
While he but small or no applause had gain'd ;
Said, he was sure my thanks you would receive
With better grace than any he could give.
'If so,' said I, 'let me, as is the vogue,
Express myself by way of Epilogue.
Pen me some lines, where I may talk and swagger
Of poisons, murders, done by bowl or dagger ;
Of Roman maids who, emulous of fame,
Have sacrificed themselves to gain a name.
Then let me step into the comic strain ;
Point out a tender nymph and dying swain,
Expose a prude, draw forth a modish wife,
And give a macaroni to the life ;
Or let me, with my brogue and action ready,
Give them a brush, my dear, of *Widow Brady.*'
'Those things,' he cried, ' would be well understood
To show your talents, not your gratitude.'
Then, as you heard, he forced me to obey,
And said—my heart must dictate what to say.
And now I pause !—Most certainly it's true,
My thanks to Wolverhampton they are due.
First for a Father, who, on this fair ground,
Has met with Friendship, seldom to be found ;
Next for his Offspring, whom your smiles have cheer'd,
And plaudits greeted whene'er she appear'd ;

A little merit, with friendly care, you spy,
When greater errors passed unnoticed by.
Would I **had** words **to** reach my wishes' height,
T' express my thankfulness to all to-night,
Yet **give** me leave most humbly to impart
The fervent feelings of a grateful heart.
May all your wants be speedily supplied,
And all your wishes happily enjoy'd ;
May th' All-good Power your every virtue nourish—
Health, wealth, and trade, in Wolverhampton flourish."

Let us leap over a few years, and as a fitting *pen-dant* to these **lines, transcribe from** the original manuscript, and print for the first time, an " Address to the town of Wolverhampton, **written** and delivered by Mr. **Henry** Siddons," the son of our tragic muse :—

" **From** lowest life, up to the highest station,
Each would *keep moving* in his own vocation ;
The crafty **cit says to** his only son,
' **Get money,** Tommy, and you must *push on !'*
The greedy courtier eager in his wishes,
Will still *keep moving* for the loaves and fishes ;
No twinge of conscience can his course prolong,
Int'rest's the word ! and, damme, *dash along !*
Behold the roaring buck the **pavement tear,**
Dash through the streets ; the crowding **vulgar stare,**
Admire his steeds—while some sagacious don
Cries, ' There's the road to ruin—so, *push on !'*
The simpering miss, when pa' has got a plum,
Neglects the shop, for opera, ball, or drum ;
Forgets her old acquaintance, simpers, leers,
And so *keeps moving* for a few short years,
Till, all her father's well-earned riches fail,
And miss still *pushes on*—into a jail !
The gallant sailor never heeds the blast,
Though **red-hot** bullets blaze about the mast ;

'*Push on !*' he cries while grappling with the foe :
'Damme, my messmates, give 'em blow for blow !'
Still may our tars, this gen'rous ardour proving,
Maintain the seas, and make our foes *keep moving !*
A few words for *myself* I now would ask :
Let me express my thanks—an arduous task ;
Yet, though my tongue refuse to do me right,
My heart *keeps moving* for my *friends* to-night :
Still may your wealth, your town, your trade improving,
Keep you still *pushing on*, while I *keep moving !*"

These kind of addresses, though driven from the London stage, are still to be heard in provincial theatres, where they obtain the wished-for applause, from the—

" *Lœtus sessor plausorque theatro.*"

Mr. Henry Siddons appeared to be the " son of his father," and not of his mother ; for he never, either in his writing or acting, rose above the rank of dull respectability. He dramatised the " Sicilian Romance " of Mrs. Radclyffe ; and it was produced at Drury Lane, May 28, 1794, for the benefit of Middleton ; so that he began to work pretty early at dramatic authorship.*
He made his first appearance at Drury Lane, as an actor, on October 8, 1801, when he performed the character of a German lawyer in a piece called " In-

* He also published a work freely adapted from the German of M. Engel, called *Practical Illustrations of Rhetorical Gesture and Action.* Some of the plates to this book are valuable, inasmuch as they represent the theatrical costumes and attitudes of his illustrious mother.

tegrity," which was believed to be his own writing ;
but it did not meet with success, and was withdrawn
after two representations.   On the 12th of October,
he had recovered from his mortification at this failure
sufficiently to essay, for the first time, the character of
Hamlet ; a character which would seem always to attract and meet with applause, even when only " respect-
ably " performed.   When Kemble first appeared at
Covent Garden, in 1803, his nephew, Mr. Henry Siddons, appeared there (together with his wife), and had
a share in the management.   Mrs. Henry Siddons
was "a lovely actress," and played Desdemona to
Kemble's Othello.

In reading the various biographies of Mrs. Siddons,
the following scraps of particulars strike us as being
both curious and noteworthy.   One of Mrs. Siddons's
favourite Shakspearian characters was Hamlet, although
she never performed it in London ; but in the pro-
vinces she played it repeatedly, and with the greatest success.   It was often the character selected for her benefit
night.   (Would that Miss Cushman would add Hamlet
to her rôle of Shakspearian delineations ; it would be a
worthy *pendant* to her Romeo.)   At other times, Mrs.
Siddons appeared as Ophelia, and brought her musical
abilities into effect, by singing the incidental songs.
When she played Imogen, in 1802, her male dress " was

exactly the strait or frock coat and trousers of our modern beaux." She personated Venus, in Garrick's "Ju-
bilee;" and, at a promenade concert, supper, and ball,
given by Brooks's Club at the Opera House, she recited
an ode in the character of Britannia, and then sat in the
attitude assumed by that merry monarch's mythological
beauty on our copper coinage! In 1792, Mrs. Siddons recited (at the Opera House) Collins's "Ode to
the Passions," to the great delight of every hearer; and
after her retirement from the stage in 1812, she revived these recitations * (at the Argyle Rooms), with
readings from Shakspeare and Milton. She died, full
of years and honour, at her house in Upper Baker
Street, London, June, 8th, 1831, aged 76.†

---

* Henderson (who was one of the first to thoroughly appreciate
the talents of Mrs. Siddons) was also in the habit of giving recitations at Freemasons' Hall, in which (says his biographer Ireland)
"he read into reputation some things which seem to have been
gathered to the dull of ancient days; and, but for such a revival,
had probably been still covered with the cloak of oblivion." The
favourite, and chief of these "revivals" was Cowper's "John Gilpin,"
which had appeared in one of the public papers, and for six years
had been comparatively unnoticed. "Mr. Henderson's very *outré*
manner of reading it" at once made it a favourite with the public, and raised it to a popularity it has never since lost, but had
never before enjoyed. John Gilpin's "diverting history" was re-
printed over and over again; one bookseller alone sold six thousand
copies of it; and its author, who had at first appeared ashamed to
acknowledge it as his own composition, now saw it recognised as a
chef-d'œuvre of humorous verse.

† With the date and place of Mrs. Siddons's birth we are not so

well acquainted; for on this point she is a very Homer to her biographers. Campbell's account is probably the correct one : that she was born at the "Shoulder of Mutton," in the town of Brecon, in South Wales; though on what day is uncertain. The 5th and 14th of July, 1755, are both given as the day of her birth, despite the Irish axiom laid down in Lover's song of "St Patrick,"

"Shure, no one should have two birth-days, but a twins."

In Tymm's Family Typographer (vol. **iv. p.** 292, 1834) we are told "at Lower Swinford (near **Stourbridge, Worcester**), a thatched cottage is shown as the birth-place of the actress Mrs. Siddons, who is said to have made her 'very **first**' *debût* in a barn at Bell Lane, at the coronation of **George** III." But this "Family Typographer" is a loose and very inaccurate work ; **and**, indeed, **its** author elsewhere tells us, that Mrs. Siddons "made **her** first *debût*" at Kington, in Herefordshire. The reader who has paid his money for Mr. **Tymm's** information can therefore take his **choice** which of these two **statements is** best (or least) deserving of credit. "Utrum horum **mavis** accipe !" virtually says the accommodating Mr. Tymms to his gentle reader.

MRS. SEPTIMUS BROWN.

Mary Johnson one day in a Brown study sat,
She'd a book in her hand, but she thought not of that,
For throughout every page, in each verb and each
    noun,
She still saw the same words—"Mrs. Septimus
    Brown."

Pit-a-pat went her heart, and, so great its pulsation,
Her stays could not stay its minutest vibration;
So she rose from her seat, and she threw her book
    down,
And yet still saw those words—"Mrs. Septimus
    Brown."

From her writing-desk then, where of treasures a
    hoard—
Hair-lockets, old trinkets, love-letters—were stored,
Some paper she took, and she just scribbled down,
Those three magic words—"Mrs. Septimus Brown."

Vastly well they appeared, and the name sounded pat,
Like a smart London footman's knock, rat-a-tat-tat,
And she said to herself "'Twill astonish the town,
To hear I'm become Mrs. Septimus Brown."

For this Mr. Brown was the luckiest of men,
Like Cæsar, he "came, saw, and conquered;" and
    then
At once popp'd the question, and she didn't frown,
But consented to be Mrs. Septimus Brown.

And he, who could woo her, and make her his wife,
Has indeed won a prize in the lottery of life;
And like a good Turk, he may swear by Mahoun,
The pattern of wives 's Mrs. Septimus Brown.

For, beauty and grace shine in feature and form,
Her heart is with tenderest sympathy warm;
While themselves in sweet bliss the Loves seem to
    drown,
In her who will be Mrs. Septimus Brown.

We will pray that all blessings may on her be shed
When the pale orange-blossom is wreathing her head,
That day when a Bride in her white satin gown,
Mary Johnson becomes Mrs. Septimus Brown.

JUPON SQUELETTE;

OR, "THE SKELETON PETTICOAT."

EGYPTIANS (says the ancient story),
   Placed skeletons at banquets, for each guest
To have before him a *memento mori,*
   That while he pick'd his bones with gourmand zest,
He might remember that, though hale and hearty,
He, too, must change into a bony party.

The world grows more refined as it grows older;
   We all should shrink from such a festal guest
Before it, e'en the freshest mirth would moulder,
   And in its presence, jokes would lose their zest :
And yet, for skeletons we have a passion,
In all assemblies of the world of fashion.

In robes *la mode* we clothe their solemn strictures
   In *toilettes* we entomb their churchyard hints ;
We dress their old bones into pretty pictures,
   Like those **La Follet** for our pastime prints.

The bony moralist becomes a charlatan,
And masquerades it in a dress of tarlatan.

Hidden 'neath heaps of petticoats and flounces,
   Eclipsed by billowy clouds of gauze and lace,
The skeleton his whereabouts announces,
   And holds his Houri in a wide embrace:
And this the warning of these Houris *may* be,—
" Bone of thy bone—thy rib—I may some day be !"

THE LITERATURE OF THE SHOP.

A COUNTRY RECTOR'S COMMENTARY.

It was just three days since; indeed, to speak
with preciseness, it was Saturday, the 4th of May.
Sophonisba, who is at once the joy and better half of
my existence, was breakfasting with me in the dining-
room of my pleasant country rectory. Within the
room everything (including our two selves), looked
agreeable, bright, and warm; out of doors it was cold
and cheerless, and anything but agreeable. Although
the almanacks assured us that we had entered upon
the genial month of May, yet, the east wind was
howling, biting, and cutting, and was altogether
behaving itself with a rude severity that no panegyric
of Mr. Kingsley could mitigate, while a driving hail-
storm rattled against the window-panes with a sound
like the dropping fire at a Volunteer Review.

"Sophonisba!" I exclaimed to the joy of my existence, as I turned from the kippered salmon to the

N

devilled kidneys (my tastes are proverbially simple), "Sophonisba, it is well that we have not sacrificed our winter garments upon the altar of our fickle climate, but have relied upon the truth of our village adage, ' Till May be out, ne'er change a clout.' If my singing curate, Motet, were with us, we could perform that pretty old glee, ' Hail, all hail, thou merry month of May ! ' it would be appropriate. Only think of the extravagance of the poets who describe the merriness of the month ! and the 'ethereal mildness' of Thomson, who could talk of '*gentle* Spring !' Poet Hood was much nearer the mark when he described the breezes of spring as resembling the blows of Spring the fighter. Perhaps, Sophonisba, you may remember the verse :—

> ' What wonder if in May itself I lack
>   A peg for laudatory verse to hang on ?
> Spring mild and gentle ? yes, as Spring-heel'd Jack,
>   To those he sprang on !
> In short, whatever panegyrics lie,
>   In fulsome odes too many to be cited,
> The tenderness of Spring is all my eye,
>   And that is blighted ! '

Hood's wit is ever blooming ; is it not, Sophonisba ? "

  . " Think of the blossoms, my dear Alphonso ! " was the response, as a fresh *feu de joie* of hail rattled against the window. " The wall-fruit is gone ; and, now, the apples will be caught."

Between mouthfuls, I was cutting the leaves of that morning's " Saturday Review," and was dipping into their article on " Negroes, and Negro Slavery ;" so, instead of vouchsafing any other intelligent reply than a grunt, I shortly called Sophonisba's attention to the Review. It so happened, that, during the previous fortnight, the greater portions of my evenings had been occupied by new books by consuls Petherick and Hutchinson, on Ethiopia and the Soudan, and by Reid's " Sketches in North America;" and these works, and the present crisis in America, had made me more than ordinarily impressible on the subject of the slave-trade. I presume that it arose from this combination of circumstances, that I suddenly uttered the Archimedean cry of *Eureka !* when, after laying aside the " Saturday Review," I had turned to glance over the various printed and lithographed communications that formed a part of the contents of that morning's letter-bag.

Now, parsons are peculiarly liable to other visitations than those of an archidiaconal character, and they are notably exposed to the literary attacks of puffing tradesmen. The chief assailants (apart from clerical subjects, appeals from Church Defence Associations, and Insurance Companies), are hatters, grocers, tailors, and wine-merchants. They are particularly attentive to me; and, unlike the generality of my brethren, I always glance over their epistolary commendations of their own wares—not with the thought of giving any order to these mercantile anglers (for I never once have risen to their most alluring flies), but solely for the enjoyment that I derived from a perusal of their literary efforts. For, it appears to me, that the literature of the shop is an astonishing evidence of the progress of education, and a distinguishing characteristic of the Victorian era. To me the development of this peculiar branch of literature seems to be a feature of the age—an useful one, probably, and remunerative, or our nation of shopkeepers would not bestow so much care or money upon it. They are no longer content to call a spade, a spade. They send it forth in mountebank disguise, with a nomenclature which is neither English, French, Greek, nor Latin, but perhaps, a base mixture of all four; and through the aid of literature, this wonderful article is recommended to notice, and puffed into a pseudo fame, by the most ingenious artifices.

De tea fabula narratur.—I might tell you a tale of a tea-merchant in our county-town, or I might cite the cases of the butcher and the two rival tailors, who every week, in the pages of our " Slowshire Independent," puff their respective goods through the medium of mor-

tal verse. I am not ashamed to confess that if I do not
use or consume their wares, I devour the verses. To
my mind, their lyrics form one of the chief attractions of the "Independent," whose articles, it must
be confessed, are not equal in ability to those in the
"Saturday Review;" and it is often a subject of
curious speculation to me—Who writes their verses?
There was the butcher's poem, last week, on the subject of Garibaldi: I vow that it had all the fire and
grace of Tupper! the delightfully easy way in which
it turned from Italy and Garibaldi to "Giblett's juicy
chops," and the delicate yet forcible manner in which
it pointed out that Giblett was no less a patriot than
Garibaldi in his endeavours to serve his countrymen,
was, to my mind, not unworthy of our great Prover-
bial Philosopher. While, in the same newspaper,
there was another poem on the subject of the British
Volunteers marching to glory in Aaron's guinea
pants, which Miss Euphemia Gushington might have
owned.

"Yes, Sophonisba!" I cried; "I never throw
these advertising circulars into the waste-paper basket
without having first extracted the honey of their style,
and made myself master of their eloquent rhetoric.
Here is another circular from the Great East Indian
Brandisherri Wine Company, enclosing quite a pretty

pamphlet on the wine trade and prospects of the
vintage, and a confidential (lithographed) letter, stating
their possession, under very peculiar circumstances, of
a pipe of a fine fruity port, which they have not thrown
into their general stock, but which they have thought-
fully reserved for their own immediate friends, who
will be privileged to purchase it for a mere bagatelle.
Now, I wonder what the bagatelle may be when translated into the simple letters £ *s. d.*; and also, whether
or no they include me among their immediate friends ;
and, if so, why?   But, here, Sophonisba, is the circular over which I cried Eureka, for it cuts the Gordian
knot—it provides us with a solution of the Sphynx's
enigma—it gives us the recipe for throwing the old
man of the sea from off our shoulders ; in short, it tells
us how to put an end to the slave trade.   So you see,
Sophonisba, that, despite your occasional surprise at
what you deem my waste of time in glancing over
these trade puffs—which are meant to swell into a trade
wind to blow custom to the advertiser—yet that I am
able to pick up nuggets of knowledge in these literary
diggings.   In harmonious and elegant prose, the
circular thus commences : it is from the Cosmopolitan
Composite and Translucent Candle Company : ' It is
but seldom that any really great improvement in manufactures is achieved.   To speak comparatively, it was

but yesterday, when cotton dipped in tallow formed
the chief candle for general use. But, at this day,
products imported from tropical climates, aided by
Science, give forth crystallized material from which the
beautiful candles now offered are obtained.' Then
follow Statistics, treated with Gladstonian skill, and
remarks on the palm-oil trade, and then comes my
Eureka. 'The development of this branch of their
manufactures will promote *the extinction of the slave-
trade.*' A sufficient reason, of course, why all these
Britons, who never will be slaves, should patronize the
Cosmopolitan Candle Company. By the way, what a
useful fact this would be for an Exeter Hall orator, for
I suppose the May Meetings extend their sympathies
to the Man and the Brother. I remember hearing a
speech on the subject, and very proper sentiments
being expressed, and I certainly thought with the
speaker, that we had no longer a right to expect
a continuance of those blessings which we have so long
enjoyed, if we in the slightest degree encouraged that
unhallowed and cruel traffic in man, against which
England, for more than fifty years, has been working
by the efforts of her greatest statesmen, and her best
and bravest sailors. Aye, Sophonisba, but there's the
rub. Look at these circulars, and all the varied literature of the shop, and see how eloquently and ingeni-

ously they commend commodities, our very use of which arises from and assists the development of the slave-trade. This puff from the candle company is, in shop-language, a startling novelty. Supposing their statement to be correct, they need not fear that it will be basely plagiarized in this circular of Carraway's, the tea-dealers. If we do not wish to encourage, in the slightest degree, that unhallowed and cruel traffic in man, we must make up our minds to deprive ourselves of a tithe (to speak rectorially) of those articles of necessity on which the literature of the shop so eloquently descants. You, Sophonisba, will have to reply to Mr. Carraway when he addresses you on the subject of sugar, that you are determined not to lend any support to the slave-trade; and I must bear the same testimony when he speaks to me of coffee. Mr. Carraway would probably think us mere Bedlamites. But we might reply to fifty other tradesmen in similar terms, and yet be in our right minds. For use has dulled our senses to facts, and if our comforts and appetites are ministered to, we are content to shut our eyes to the means employed. I have quite done now, Sophonisba; and am going into the study to write my sermon."

"My dear Alphonso," said the joy of my existence, "I think you have been preaching one to me."

FANNY'S MIRROR.

"VELUTI IN SPECULUM."

WOULD that I were Fanny's mirror!
   I should see her half the day;
She would then be loath to leave me,
   She would love with me to stay.
With her merry eyes of hazel,
   She would peer into my face;
Oh! that I and Fanny's mirror,
   For a day could change our place.

Oh! if I were Fanny's mirror,
   She would show me all her charms,
Rosy cheeks, and lips of coral,
   Snowy neck, and rounded arms.
She, without a moment's blushing,
   All her beauties would lay bare;
Oh! in place of Fanny's mirror,
   Would that I could then be there!

Yet, if I were Fanny's mirror,
  I should see her with new eyes;
For, she then would stand before me
  Maskless, and without disguise.
There would then be no coquetting,
  Save a bit for practice' sake;—
Shall I, then, of Fanny's mirror
  Ever wish to take the place?

No!—if I were Fanny's mirror,
  May-be she would cease to charm;
Made-up smiles, and practised blushes,
  Real attractions would disarm.
Ignorance is bliss; rehearsals
  Please not like the acted play;—
So, let me and Fanny's mirror
  In our wonted places stay.

THE OLD TOMB IN THE ABBEY.

Amid the pride, and pomp, and state,
 That wait upon King Death; amid the splendour
That loads the last beds of the great,
 And deadens in the heart each feeling tender,
To see the solemn grave bedeck'd
 With sculptured marble, and with gold,
 While he who lies there dead and cold,
Had all his hopes of heaven wreck'd;
Amid the false-born pride of birth—
 The fulsome epitaphs that seem
To show man's mind is all on earth,
 His thoughts of heaven but a dream—
Amid these proud memorials is a tomb,
 Which stands a silent monitor to those around,
Scarce seen amid the murky gloom
 Its mightier brethren cast upon the marble ground.

'Tis but a slab—time-eaten—trodden under foot—
 Unornamented—but a simple stone;

And yet, like Memnon's statue, though 'tis mute,
  There seems a very breath, a murmur'd tone
To breathe from out it, as it were a voice
That bids the mourning mother to rejoice.
It lies unheeded by the careless crowd,
  For, 'tis to one whose life is undefiled,
And tells not of the mighty nor the proud,—
  Its epitaph these simple words—" 𝔇𝔢𝔞𝔯𝔢 𝔠𝔥𝔦𝔩𝔡𝔢." *

How beautiful, how touching, how sincere !
  How grand, yet humble—simple, yet how fine !
No wonder that unbidden springs the tear—
  A mother's love is hallow'd in that line :
The words are simple, but they speak unto the sense
With all the might and majesty of eloquence.

And who shall tell the mother's wild despair ?
Her silent, sleepless grief ? her tender care ?
Her deep concentred love ? her hopes and fears ?
Her wakeful watchings through the too-short years ?
Her looking on that death-paled face ?
  That late on her with joy had smiled ?
Her wish to share its dwelling-place ?—
  'Tis figured in those words—" 𝔇𝔢𝔞𝔯𝔢 𝔠𝔥𝔦𝔩𝔡𝔢."

* A tomb with this inscription may be seen in Westminster
Abbey.

THE AGREEABLE MONK.

My Agreeable Monk is no mediæval monastic with
serge gown and knotted cord; and the nearest approach
that he ever makes to such a costume is when he takes
his ease in his rich figured dressing-gown tied about
with a bell-pull.   And yet, in his aptitude for hilarity
and good living, is he like to those monks of old, who
sang, and laughed, and the rich wine quaffed, and lived
on the daintiest fare.   But my Agreeable Monk has
not yet reached to his mediæval age, not having been
born until this present century had quite run out of
its teens; and though, like the gentlemen just alluded
to, he very frequently laughs ha! ha! with a hearti-
ness that is infectious, yet I may venture to say, that
he so far comes short of his models in that he has
never quaffed ha! ha! the recipe for that peculiar
beverage having been lost in the mediæval mists.

My Agreeable Monk, too, has no circular spot
shaven upon the top of his crown, a veritable crown-
piece gleaming like silver from its dark boundary of

hair; neither has he smoothly-shaven jesuitical cheeks, such as we meet with on the countenances of theatrical gentlemen, Popish priests, and other actors, where the blueness of the mown surface interposes with marked effect between the red and white of cheek and choker. On the contrary, my Agreeable Monk can boast a capillary development of hyacinthine locks, and whiskers that are only tamed down from a militant air, by being trimmed and curled to the meekness of the lady-killer.   No recluse or ascetic is he, but a "muscular Christian;" still able, if need be, to use his fists in self-defence; still vigorous to pull an oar; still ready to ride across country whenever he can frame an excuse for a "short cut;" and with his lungs still in a highly-healthy condition to bear their part in secular glees or to chant the service in —————— Cathedral.   For, in a Minor degree, he is one of its dignitaries; and, within its timeworn precincts, possesses a snug monastic retreat, admirably adapted to modern tastes and ideas.

It lies hard by the sacred building.   The giant shadow of the great central tower steals over it in the summer's sunset; and the prebendal rooks and jackdaws take it under their protection as an important portion of ecclesiastical property.   We go round by the Lady Chapel, by a broad walk between level plots

of turf, and **passing under** a low, dark, groined arch-
way, find ourselves in **cool grey cloisters, enclosing a**
square **green lawn** bright with flower-knots, on which
we gaze through the unglazed windows.   Pleasant **is**
it on a **July** day to struggle out of the glaring sunshine
into the refreshing retreat of these cool cloisters—to
pace their paved walks on their northern and western
sides, and watch the golden light glowing on the other
sides of the square, bringing out into all the sharpness
of shine and shade **the bright flower-knots, the creep-**
ing masses **of ivy, the mullioned windows, and but-**
tresses, and battlements, and **warming up** the queer
old Gargoyles into fresh leers and laughter.

Along a shady side, and then we **step into** patches
of sunlight ; and after passing some half dozen doors
(but **no windows)** we come to a portal whose formidable
look of united oak and **iron** is considerably enlivened
by a door-plate and letter-box in the newest style of
mediæval enrichment.   Fascinated by the gay colours,
we peruse the rubric **legends, and, trout-like, swallow**
the bait.   A tug, and we are **hauled within, and in a**
trice are landed **in the domains of our Agreeable**
Monk.

An oak-panelled **hall,** matted under **foot.**   On one
wall, the Oxford Almanack, mediævally framed ; on   —
the other side, over a Gothic oak hall-table, a framed and

emblazoned list of anthems and cathedral services for the week. Hard by, over-coats, boating-hats, chimney-pot-hats, and college-caps; then surplices and hoods, pendant from the wall, where at night, as I walk by them, they look like the ghosts of murdered minor-canons. And (Nota Bene!) not far from them a cupboard lurking beneath the stairs; and, within it, a goodly store of pipes and tobacco. Down the hall, and to the further end of a passage, and we pass through a door.

A tolerably large and lofty room, of collegiate character, luxurious, and comfortable. The doors are of panelled oak, with ecclesiastical handles and hinges; there are two tall mullioned windows, filled with sheets of plate-glass; and there is an enormous fireplace, with steel dogs, and shining encaustic tiles, and a black oak chimney-piece nearly touching the ceiling, rich in carved work, relieved with gilding, and gay with a double row of emblazoned coats-of-arms. The walls are papered with a light sea-green, diapered with dark green fleur-de-lys; the window-curtains are now a thin white muslin, but in colder weather marone, with a broad gold border of a Greek pattern; the carpet a soft Turkey, on which the footfalls die a Desdemona death. Thickly hung upon the walls are proof-prints from world-famed pictures by Raffaelle and Ary Scheffer, interspersed with large photographs of English and Continental Cathedrals, and with a few masterly water-colours. They are hung in frames of gold, and velvet, and carved oak ; and, as they all have wide white margins, they show out with telling effect from the sea-green walls. The book-cases are of light polished woods, carved in places with open work, behind which dark green cloth has been introduced ; green leather, stamped with a gold pattern, is hung from the shelves, which are laden with richly-bound books, redolent of russia, and magnificent with morocco. In one corner is a stand for portfolios and prints ; opposite to it is a Collard's semi-grand, on which the Agreeable Monk will by-and-by discourse most excellent music. Dotted about everywhere are various species of the *genus* chair—Glastonbury chairs, lounging chairs, easy chairs, that do not belie their name, and stiff-backed chairs, for ornament (it is to be presumed) and not for penance. Then, there are two or three tables, where are newspapers, and some of the latest periodicals and reviews, and a miscellaneous oddment of the current sacred and profane literature, stacked for convenience of reference (with a Peerage, and a Clergyman's Almanac, and a Gardening Calendar, and a Book of Anthems, and a Clergy List, and Army List, and Navy List, and other handy books) in oak book-stands with carved ends of shields and fleur-de-lys. And, in a well-lighted corner, is a writing-table,—so well appointed that it is a pleasure to sit down to it, and scribble off a whole week's arrears of correspondence. From the cushioned recesses of the two windows, we can look out on the flower-pots of a trimly-kept garden, shaded by venerable limes and cedars. Those sweet blossomy limes are a very store-house of enjoyment for the Agreeable Monk's bees, who are grandly lodged in yonder ecclesiastical summer-house, the Gothic carvings of which were constructed "out of his own head," as was once observed by a jocose prebendary, adopting the witty saying of another jocose prebendary, in order to make mild fun out of the Agreeable Monk's amateur carpenterings.　And there, against the south wall of the garden, with the Cathedral towers o'ertopping the elms for a background to the view, there is a conservatory filled with floral beauties, to whom the Agreeable Monk makes himself as benevolently amiable as though he were the Lady of the Sensitive Plant.

What a charming snuggery it is, lacking nothing but a wife to make it perfect; though, if the hundred tongues of Rumour speak the truth (and, for a wonder, they are unanimous on this point), an Eve is soon to appear in this Paradise, and the Monk will have to break his celibate vow.　There is room for *her*, at any rate; for are there not two sitting-rooms downstairs, and two bed-rooms with dressing-rooms upstairs? So let her come and welcome; and as for the future (as Horace says), don't ask what fate is going to bestow upon you. At present the Agreeable Monk's nursery is in his garden.

As for domestic arrangements,—besides a boy in buttons, of preternatural sharpness, who is his own peculiar slavey,—there are male and female servants to obey his wants, in common with those of his five other companions who may happen to be "in residence." Their homes all lie in these cloistered courts, and they form a corporation of their own, as the aforesaid jocose prebendary observed, when he directed attention to the increasing rotundity in the form of one of the reverend gentlemen; and they have their own lands and proper- ties, and are mighty big folk accordingly.

My Agreeable Monk—in anticipation, I suppose, of the coming change in his condition,—has thought fit to convert a room, on the opposite side of the cloistered quad, into a kitchen, that is as unlike to an ordinary kitchen as the Agreeable Monk is to an anchorite of old. For, besides its mullioned windows and carved stone fire-place, its walls are curiously ornamented like a parquetted floor, while the floor itself is laid with encaustic tiles. Not that there is any urgent need for this glorified kitchen; for is there not the great kitchen common to the six cloistered monks, from whence, at the word of command, as with the waving of a magic wand, all the wonders of cookery will arise. But my Agreeable Monk likes to do things on the grand seigneur scale; and, I daresay, when dinner time comes, instead of letting us enjoy our *tête-à-tête* in that snug dining-room of his (whose only offensive decoration is that too-popular print of the Three Impossible Choristers—their appearance here to be excused on the ground of association and sublimation of ideas), he will haul me up to the other end of the cloisters, up the grand staircase, and into the great dininghall (in which, to quote the jocose prebendary, he and his corporation have a vested interest), where I shall not be surprised to find covers laid for a score. Nor shall I wonder if, later in the evening, we adjourn to the music-room, where, arrayed in awful state in the orchestra, he and his *confrères* will fiddle me either into Elysium or into the land of Nod.

How, as I lounge in a luxurious chair in that light, and pleasant, and thoroughly liveable room of his— how I marvel at the Agreeable Monk, as he roves from sweet to sweet of his charming home—now mounting his music-stool to play ponderous Gregorians, or heathenish waltzes—now exhibiting, with a collector's *gusto*, a rare black-letter, or choice Caxton—now dart-

ing into his garden to remove a snail from the Duchess
of Sutherland, or some withered leaves from the Souvenir de Malmaison—now taking me up-stairs to his
workshop, amid the big beams of the high pitched roof
where he has a lathe and all other carpenter's tools,
and where he saws me out a shield, and turns me a
tobacco-stopper, while I note the Rembrandt effect of
the sunbeams streaming through the narrow mullions
of the dormer windows, and barely lighting the odd
lumber of the quaint room.

By-and-by I am carried off to the coach-houses and
stables, where an episcopal-looking cob whinnies a
How-d'ye-do, and a Dandie Dinmont rushes at us with
frantic caresses. Then, Dandie Dinmont leading the
way, we pass on to the fruit and kitchen-garden, slop-
ing down to the river's edge, where the centre walk
terminates in a flight of steps descending to the water.
Moored close beside the steps is what is called by the
poets " a light shallop," but by mortals a pleasure-boat,
into which Dandie jumps and we step ; and, presently,
cool and comfortable in his shirt sleeves, the Agreeable
Monk is pulling me up the stream,—I steering, and
Dandie keeping a sharp look-out a-head. So, up the
river for a mile or so, and then turn, dropping quietly
down with the stream—the rich meadows on either
hand, with cattle, and clumps of trees—and before us

the quaint old city, with its bridges and cathedral towers. And while we gaze, the bells begin to softly chime for afternoon prayer; and so we moor the boat and stable Dandie.

Ere the last vibrations of the chimes have quivered upon the ripples of the air, the surplice of the Agreeable Monk has fluttered through the private cloister that connects his own quad with the southern transept of the cathedral, and he is in his own proper stall, and I not far distant. Then I hear once more that grand Service, that daily, for centuries, has led the worship of God in one long song of most triumphant praise. Then we return through the private cloister, and linger in its cool precincts to note its old oak roof, whose beams are so curiously carved with birds, and beasts, and fishes, and Noah going into the ark, and **Joseph's** dream of the sheaves, and the spies bearing the fruit of the Promised Land. The next morning I hear the cathedral Service again, but from a novel quarter—the room over the north transept.

It is a large and lofty room; so large, that it covers the whole of the spacious transept; so lofty, that its groined roof is high enough for a church. It has but **two** windows at its north end; it is true that they are very large **windows**, but their glass quarries are encrusted with a century's accumulation of dirt and

cobwebs; and, therefore, the light that struggles
through them is **certainly dim, and** may possibly **be
religious** also.

Scattered around **the room, are** cases and chests,
clamped and bound with iron and profusely padlocked :
they are outwardly covered with dust, and inwardly
crammed with ancient deeds and registers, and nobody
knows what. Standing about on the dark oak floor
—tall, attenuated, and gaunt, the very ghosts **of woe-**
begone bookcases—are numerous **old presses, containing**
more numerous, and still older, **books. The** presses
are very shabby **in their outward seeming ; the books**
still more so. Yet, as **in life, those squalid,** shabby-
looking cases have bright and good contents, that **can**
make sunshine in many a dark spot, and cheer many
a sad hour. These gaunt and shabby presses are so
many armouries for books ; **for, every** book within
them has its sides protected by plates **of metal—**
breastplates that have guarded them from the onslaught
of damp, and have warded off **many a** piercing thrust
from grub and worm. They **are also a very Tyburn**
for books ; for every book **is hung** in chains, like
culprit volumes that have been gibbeted for their evil
deeds ; and it is far from impossible but what they
may, in their time, have murdered many a fact and
reputation. These chains are long and rusty, and are

made to slide upon iron rods that run the whole length
of the presses, and are then fastened with a padlock;
and at the end of each press is a book-desk.

Even now, as I gaze upon my friend's Library, I
can fancy that I see the old monks taking down their
Chrysostom, or Cyprian, or the " Canones Apostolici,"
or the " Liber Sacerdotalis," or the " Corpus Juris
Canonici," or the " Codex Canonum Ecclesiæ Uni-
versæ," or the " Hesychii Lexicon Græcè," or the
" Summa Summæ" of Thomas Aquinas, or any other
book of reference, or history, or devotional exercise,
and laying it upon the book-shelf within length of
the chain, the while they turned to some passages, and
perhaps made a mark for future reference, by picking
up one of the reeds from the rush-strewn floor and
placing it between the leaves: and lo, to make my
fancy more life-like, as I turn over the leaves of the
chained books, I come upon many of these monkish
markers—dry reeds that, as I touch them, crumble
into the dust, to which they who placed them there
have long since turned. And I can fancy those old
monks, wishful to read further in their own cloistered
cell, their " Polycarpi Epistola," or " Bedæ Opera,"
or " Bibliotheca Patrum," and applying for a loan of
the volume to the Librarian, who would slide the chain
to the end of the bar, unlock the padlock, lift up the

bar, slip the chain from off it, and deliver over the book to the applicant.

I can fancy all this. In my imagination, I can see those monks of old thus reading, and thus taking down, those gibbeted books. But the Agreeable Monk I see doing it in reality: and, while I look over some rare manuscripts, and marvel at the wonderful labour bestowed upon them, with their brilliant illuminations as clear and vivid as though painted yesterday, and their grotesque biblical illustrations (yet withal so valuable to the archæologist and artist), in which King Pharaoh, in an embroidered surcoat and Milan suit of armour of the time of Richard the Second, is pursuing Israelites, who wear tabards, with hats, and scrips, and staves, like Chaucer's poor ploughman—and who are embossed and touched up with gold, in a manner we wot not of,—while I look at these glorified manuscripts, and speculate against the probabilities of the amateur artists, their authors, producing more than one such work in an average lifetime, the Agreeable Monk, my friend, takes off his coat, and pursues his beloved (and gratuitous) work of arranging, and preserving, and collating, and mending, and patching, and binding, and, in short, rescuing from general oblivion and destruction these marvellous volumes which were once so deservedly prized, and have for so many years been wantonly neglected. Already has he discovered more than one volume that is supposed to be unique; and has brought to light others that the British Museum would willingly purchase for a very large sum.

As we pursue our respective occupations—he, blowing clouds of dust, and rusting his hands, and rattling his chains, like a very Bibliomaniac as he is,—I, poring over a very fleshy Moses being taken out of very verdant bulrushes by a doll-faced lady attired in the horned head-dress of Henry the Fifth,—while we are thus buried in meditation and clouds of dust, the cathedral service is going on down below, and the waves of sound float into our dim old chamber, and waft our thoughts to the haven where they would be.

And thus, amid these sights and sounds, I sit, and gaze, and listen, and dream,—dreams that are only interrupted by the rattling of the old rusty chains, when my companion bestows his duteous care on another gibbeted volume. May that, his labour of love, be his least worthy monument!

But whenever I see his name in print, and, affixed thereto, those mystic letters that signify his University Rank, I take those two simple letters, A.M., to stand not for plain " Master of Arts," but for " Agreeable Monk."

THE HANGMAN'S SHOW.

NOTE.—The two following advertisements appeared in the *Birmingham Daily Mercury*, June 13, 1856 :—

PALMER'S EXECUTION.

A GOOD VIEW of the DROP, from a firm and secure Platform, erected within a few yards of the Scaffold, may be obtained by applying to Joseph Darlington, Currier's Arms Inn, Sash-street, Stafford.

N.B.—*This Platform will be close to one erecting to contain all the principal Nobility.*

Tickets, 1s. 6d. to 2s. 6d.

A GOOD PLATFORM will be **ERECTED** within a few yards of the Scaffold, thereby affording a good View of the Execution, and, being surveyed by the proper town officer, will **secure** persons wishing to witness this awful ceremony from fear of accident.

Tickets may be obtained by applying to Thomas Stanley, Builder, Stafford.

N.B.—*Accommodation separate for ladies.*

A CROWD of Christian people,
    At half-a-crown a-head,
Swarm'd on commodious platforms
    To see the Poisoner dead.

And the principal Nobility
   (If advertisements spake the truth)
Gave an air of extreme gentility
   To that moral lesson for youth.

Nob and Snob were assembled,
   Tag-rag and Bob-tail were there;
High and Low saw the Hangman's Show
   Set in Execution Fair.
And—so thoughtful the Hangman's trade is!
   Newspapers gave information,
That platforms were there for the Ladies
   With "separate accommodation."

Close were they to the scaffold,
   They could feel the Poisoner's breath
As he mounted the steps that brought him
   To his Upas-tree of Death:
To the Poisoner's tree whose shadow
   Fell with a poisoner's blight,
On the half-crown Nob, and the crowd-crush'd Snob
   Impatient to see the sight.

'Tis the Poisoner's end, in Java,
   To be shot with a poison'd dart,
Whose venom, like molten lava,
   Burns its death-way to the heart.

So, with cries and fierce convulsions,
   Ends his wretched life of pollution ;
A tragedy of repulsion —
   A dramatic " Retribution."

Oh ! if the Hangman had been
   Alive to dramatic art,
He'd have changed the cord, and cap,
   For a strychnine-poison'd dart !
Tetanic spasm and throe,
   And a lingering passage to Hades,
More attractive had made the Show
   To the two-and-sixpenny Ladies !

Let us hope, however, that they
   Had the worth of each bright half-crown ;
And that Nob and Snob, and Tag-rag, and Bob,
   Pleasure-surfeited left the town.
Yet, oh ! my christian friend,
   May it ne'er be my lot, or thine,
To witness so fearful an end,
As was seen by those who their way did wend,
   As pilgrims, to Palmer's shrine.

MURDER WORSHIP.

(NOVEMBER, 1849.)

ANOTHER blossom on the Tyburn-tree;
   And yet another on its fruitful bough !
   The murd'rers* pay their bloody reck'ning now,
And thousands throng admiringly to see.
And who shall blame the unschool'd mob, whilst we,
   The Scholars, Law's grim tragedy allow,
   Nor interest in its actors disavow.
We chronicle the foul minutiæ
Of their dark deeds of crime;—nay, stop not here,
   But sift their very prison-life, and draw
The veil from off their hidden histories !
We crowd to see their waxen effigies;
We make their portraits household gods, and rear
   Them shrines, where Murder-worship is allow'd by
   Law.

                * The Mannings.

ETERNAL WAGGONERS.

OUR waggoners are not of the Peter Bell kind,—as lovers of Wordsworth might at first imagine ; they are not the heroes of a poem which consumes twenty years of labour before it is fitted (in the opinion of its sanguine author) " for filling *permanently* a station, however humble, in the literature of our country ;" * they cannot take their places side by side with this Peter, whom the philosophic poet evidently imagined would be a permanent hero—an eternal waggoner. No ! *our* waggoners are not of this description ; they have nothing to do with a " primrose by a river's brim ;" and they are not in the habit of meeting with " a solitary ass " who possesses the accomplishment of " grinning." All such worthy people as these we leave to Wordsworth,

> " To show with what complacency he creeps
> With his dear ' Waggoners' around his lakes." †

Our " Eternal Waggoner " is nothing more nor less

* Preface to " Peter Bell."   † "Don Juan," III., 98.

than that respectable bird the Night Raven, whose
character has been so much defamed by omen-seekers
and lovers of the marvellous, and to whom the Germans
gave the peculiar *soubriquet* which heads this paper.
They have further assigned to him this singular legend:—He wished, for his share of Heaven, to drive
to all eternity; and, he accordingly drives without
cessation, sitting on the middle horse of the celestial
wain, of which the four large stars behind are the four
wheels; but the three foremost stars which stand in a
crooked line, are the three horses; and the little star,
over the middle horse, is the Eternal Waggoner. He
guides the horses, and, as the waggon always goes in
a circle, they do not stand in a right line with one another, but in a curve,—being always on the turn. Before midnight the waggon is said to be going out,—
when the pole inclines upwards; and, after midnight,
the waggon " goes home," and then the pole inclines
downwards.

Whatever could possess our Eternal Waggoner with
such a spirit of Jehu-ism, we are not informed: but it
is clear that Phaeton was not worthy to handle the
ribbons with him; while his system of driving,—the
sitting on the middle horse of a team of three,—is remarkable, not only for its simplicity, but, also, for its
daring originality.

These " Eternal Waggoners" play a leading part in many a ghostly drama, and appear upon their peculiar *stage* in a way which the lover of superstitious horrors is not slow to applaud. There, the ravens strut and fret through the witching hours of night, and gravely hop through their *pas diabolique*,—which we may be allowed to call, in reference to their " Waggoner" title, the *pas de* Carter! and they croak their Waggoners' songs in notes, which even Mdlle. Johanna Wagner would strive in vain to imitate. As it would transgress the limits of this paper, were I to follow Cap'en Cuttle's advice, and " make a note of" all the legends in which I have found the Night Raven to be a conspicuous actor, I shall here confine my notes to one or two *stories* told in connection with the Eternal Waggoners of my native County, Worcestershire.

In the fairy-haunted parish of Alfrick, on the confines of hop-growing Herefordshire, there is a sandy lane leading by Patch Hill to Bridge's Stone, and past " the Fairy's Cave ;" and this lane is variously haunted. But we must not stop to notice the spectral, black greyhound ; nor must we even dwell upon the shadowy waggon with its coal-black team ; for the waggoner of whom we are now about to speak has no connection with this vehicle, any more than that it passes the house wherein he lives. It is in an old cider house that the

Eternal Waggoner has fixed his abode, and there he always sits, perched upon a barrel, of which he constitutes himself the sole proprietor; for should any unfortunate wight be presumptuous enough to endeavour to help himself to the contents of the barrel, the Eternal Waggoner forthwith flies at him, and flouts him with its wing, until he runs away, terrified and ciderless.

Why a raven should be chosen as the peculiar ghostly custos of a cider or beer-barrel, I cannot say; though I am inclined to believe that the proprietor of a beer or cider-barrel may find that an Eternal Waggoner, or any other harmless bird for whom a rustic servant may feel a superstitious horror, is a better preservative for the barrel's contents, than all the locks, bolts, and bars that were ever affixed to cellar doors. The gentle reader may depend upon it, that if his ale-cask loses its fulness of body by a mysterious system of evaporation, for which even the all-destructive "cat" may not be blamed, he cannot do better than get a good ghost astride the cask! Once induce an Eternal Waggoner to perch there, and your malt liquor will be secure from depredation.

The fact is, that the agricultural intellect is slow to recognize any charms in our Eternal Waggoner, save those charms that belong to a witchery of a very dis-

agreeable character. The Bœotian understanding of
your true clod will most readily accept as truth, any
rhodomontade which has been worked up by supernatural machinery; and will believe in any ridiculous
story so long as a bird, or beast, of ill omen figures as
a chief character. "Such dark articles of belief," as
Mr. Broderip says,* "are rapidly fading away before
the glare of gas, the rush of railroads, and the gallop
of intellect; but they still hold their sway in quiet
nooks of quiet counties." And if you were to say to a
rustic,

> "Harke! the ravenne flappes hys wynges
> In the briered delle below;" †

—especially if you could convey into the words all this
mysterious spell of spelling—your rural friend would
no more dream of sauntering with his Phyllis into that
briered dell, than he would of celebrating his Phyllis
in love verses, like the Latin rustics of the classic
times.

The cellar of **Holt Castle** (near Witley) boasts
another Eternal Waggoner, who keeps watch and ward
over the beer barrels; and whose fame is only rivalled
by that of the black lady, who takes her nightly
promenade in the attics above: the Castle being thus,
literally, haunted from top to bottom.

* "Zoological Recreations." First Series.
† Chatterton's "Mynstrelle's Songe," in "Ælla, a tragical enter-
lude."

The "rush of railroads" above alluded to—though advantageous on the whole, yet, as applied to the line between Kidderminster and Worcester, fails in some respects, when compared with those pair-horse coaches which used to drag their slow length along between "the faithful City" and the town of carpets.   For example: the coach passenger had no sooner left Kidderminster, than he passed close to the old sandstone tower (the sole survivor of four brothers) of Caldwall Castle, of which the railroad passenger does not catch a glimpse.   And thereby, the railroad passenger, very probably, fails to hear the following legend. At the base of that old crumbling tower there is an arched vault, ribbed, and rich in corbels; and out of this vault (says the legend) there is an underground passage, which leads to St. Mary's Church, and is therefore nearly a half mile long.   Perhaps this passage may have been constructed by the old monks who inhabited the Saxon monastery, on the site of which the castle was built; perhaps, Earl Cynebert may have made it, or else King Cador—who, according to the ballad, had such a strong desire to kiss the "pretty maid"*—may have used the passage in order to get to

* King Cador saw a pretty maid.
  King Cador would have kiss'd her;
  But the pretty maid slipt aside and fled;
  And so, King Cador miss'd her.

And hence (say imaginative people) the town was called "Cador-

church in a quiet and retired way. Of course there was an underground passage, or else it would never have found its way into the legend. Well, in this passage, just about midway between the castle and the church (pray let us be particular !), there is an immense chest crammed full of untold sums of gold, which, of course, has disturbed many persons to that degree, that they have not been able to rest until they have had a look at the treasure. So they have made their way to the chest, and there they have seen, perched upon the lid, an Eternal Waggoner ; and he has so terrified them, that they have always taken to their heels, and forgotten to look into the chest; so that I am, therefore, unable to state the exact amount of wealth it may contain. I have often been in the vaulted cellar beneath the tower, but I was never able to find the entrance to the subterranean passage : if I had lighted upon it, I should then, doubtless, have been enabled to give a full description of the appearance of the Eternal Waggoner,— for I *must* have seen him, because he sits there day and night—the sleepless guard of the hidden treasure.

miss'd-her ;" from whence the transition to Keder-mist-her, and from that, to Kidderminster, is both easy and obvious. But it could not be very agreeable to King Cador to have his *faux pas* thus celebrated.

THE LADY AND THE SPANIELS.

Being a modern Pythagorean's account of the well-known engraving from the picture by Sir Edwin Landseer.

READING a Sonnet to her praise,
    And lying on a velvet pillow,—
The summer ocean all a-blaze
    With sunbeams on each throbbing billow;

The sky, in colour like the hue
    Upon the Speedwell's deep blue flower;
The jess'mine odours stealing through
    The open lattice of the bower;

Soft curtains dimming those hot gleams
    The July sun is fiercely shedding,
The while the drowse of mid-day seems
    Its lazy languor o'er her spreading;

Spreading its languor over all—
　O'er Lady, lounging and luxurious,—
O'er lap-dog, curl'd into a ball,
　Yet wide awake with aspect curious.

Three Spaniels, well-bred, sleek, and dear
　To that fair maid as friends, and fór toys;
King Charles lies on the table, near
　That quaint pincushion like a tortoise.

The Blenheim by her pillow'd head,
　His shiny satin coat is sunning,
And, crouching on his velvet bed,
　Keeps watch and ward with eyes of cunning.

But, where the hyacinthine veins
　In tiny streamlets vaguely flowing—
Like marble tinged with faint blue stains—
　Are on her bosom's-broad map, showing,—

There, where her tender maiden's breast
　Would seem all ease of heart to nourish,—
Where the bright heart's-ease flower doth rest,
　And in congenial clime doth flourish,—

There, looking up with loving eyes,
　And resting on that pleasant pillow,
Her pet of pets securely lies,
　His *bark* upon her bosom's billow.

A sight that tempts us to revive
  A curious creed of old-world teaching,
Could we be certain to arrive
  At something better than mere preaching ;

At something more than empty terms
  That place the fable where the fact is,—
At ripen'd fruit, not flow'ry germs,—
  And put our precepts into practice ;

The creed Pythagoras composed, ·
  And taught to other would-be Daniels ;
That, when men's mortal lives were closed,
  Their souls might pass to such sleek Spaniels.

And, monstrous though this creed we think,
  That, at a long life's termination,
Our spiritual part could sink
  To quadrupedal degradation ;—

That, Lambs could take the Tiger's shape ;
  And Maccaronis merge in Monkeys ;
And Brutus pass into an Ape ;
  And Witlings vanish into Donkeys ;

And Gourmands grow to greedy Pigs ;
  Poll-parrots come from Politicians ;
Magpies, from Tories, Rads., and Whigs ;
  And quacking Ducks from grave Physicians ;

Yet, looking at that pet of pets,
  One's fancy grows Pythagoræan,
Its tune to transmigration sets,
  And to chimæras chaunts its pæan.

For who upon that pet could gaze,
  Without one passing thrill of pleasure
To make his passion-fire to blaze,
  His pulse to bound to livelier measure ?

Who would not, for a moment, try
  That doctrine of metempsychosis,
If, thus transform'd, he then could lie
  Where that dear dog's intrusive nose is ?

Who would not, for a moment, change
  For Samian creed his best ambition,
To be allow'd so free a range,
  And pass to that sleek pet's position ?

O happy dog ! more blest than all
  The crowd of suitors who'd displace thee,
Pythagoras, himself might call
  Supremely blest, from there to chase thee.

O lucky dog ! what blissful fate
  Has placed thee on that throbbing breast there !
Who would not change his mortal state
  For thine, if then he thus could rest there ?

Content I'd be with woes to fight,
    Content with carking cares to wrestle,
If, to that bosom warm and white,
    Like that dear dog, I thus could nestle!

Content I'd with privation rest,
    Content, with hardships harsh I'd struggle,
If, to the comfort of that breast,
    Like that dear dog I thus could snuggle!

Vain such a wish! which but begets
    In human worms cold-blooded strictures;
Yet, still, the Lady and her Pets,
    I'll prize as prettiest of my pictures.

THE HALL AND COTTAGE DOOR

ON CHRISTMAS-EVE.

'Tis Christmas Eve, and, far and wide,
  The shining snow spreads o'er the plain;
The Fairy Frost has deftly dried
  Her crystal mosses on the pane;
From grey church towers the Virgin chimes *
  O'er hill and dale their sweetness pour,
And children sing their carol rhymes
  Alike at Hall and Cottage door.

The eaves are hung with icy spars,
  Snow-wreathes fantastic forms assume,
The moon shines bright, and golden stars
  In Heaven's great garden burst to bloom;
The mansion wide its portals throws,
  As in the merry days of yore;
And Welcome sits amid the snows,
  Alike at Hall and Cottage-door.

    * The old name for the chimes on Christmas Eve.

The light that streams from lordly panes,
    And makes the painted windows burn,
Is answer'd back from lowly lanes,
    Where children hail their sire's return.
The wild bells ring with Christmas mirth,
    And tell their tale of holy lore,—
Glory on high, goodwill on earth,—
    Alike at Hall and Cottage door.

Aye ! this the key-note Christmas gives
    To cheer us through the twelvemonth long,
And tune the burden of our lives
    To echo back the angels' song.
Oh ! may we join that glorious band,
    When, earthly joys and struggles o'er,
Dwellers in Hall and Cot shall stand,
    On equal terms, at Heaven's door.

OUT!

Not many evenings ago, I had the honour to partake of the refreshment of dinner at the table of Sir Topham Sawyer, "Bart.," as Mr. Bucket would add; and I had the additional honour of being placed next to Mrs. Marker Pepps (Sir Topham's sister), whom, indeed, I had taken into the dining-room. On the other side of Mrs. Pepps sat the Rev. Mr. Lamb, the curate of the parish (Pittington, Sir Topham's country-seat), to whom the lady was graciously pleased to throw some fragments of her conversation.

These fragments of Mrs. Pepps' conversational banquet, and the observations which they educed from the reverend gentleman, were not altogether lost upon me, as I was prevented from carrying on a dialogue with old Lady Bellwether (who sat to my left) on account of the infirmity of deafness, with which that venerable lady is afflicted; and, as there was a hushed funereal tone about the repast, I could not fail to hear

the few remarks which Mrs. Marker Pepps condescended to make to her right-hand neighbour. I could
not but perceive, too, that her observations seemed to
be dictated by a spirit of curious inquiry which is
not altogether foreign to the female sex, and plays a
prominent part in the history of Blue Beard. Thus,
for instance, she interrogated Mr. Lamb as to his
county, his father's "place," his father's occupation,
and his knowledge of the So-and-Soes and other
county families; and, when she had satisfied herself
on these points, she inquired of the reverend gentleman if he had any sisters.

Mr. Lamb's reply intimated that he was blessed
with four sororial relatives, all of whom were of
tenderer years than himself—gushing Lambkins growing gracefully into Muttonhood.

Upon receiving these statistics of his family, Mrs.
Marker Pepps made this note and query: "Four
sisters have you? Oh!—are they OUT?"

"Not all of them," replied Mr. Lamb; "only the
two eldest. They came out last year."

"Indeed!" remarked Mrs. Pepps, as though the
Curate had risen fifty per cent. in her estimation.
"Last season, did they? I don't remember their
names. Who introduced them?"

The reverend gentleman appeared to be slightly

confused, as he replied, "I misunderstood you. My sisters are *not* out,—at least, in the sense that you mean."

"Oh!" said Mrs. Pepps, with an air as though the Curate had *fallen* fifty per cent. in her estimation. And, without wasting more of her colloquial banquet on a person whose sisters had come "out" in a manner which she could not be expected to recognize, she transferred her attention to the ice which was just then brought round; and, during the quarter of an hour which elapsed previous to the ladies retiring to the drawing-room, she made what observations she condescended to make to an individual who shall be nameless.

But, as that individual bent over his ice, and thought what a capital refrigerator Mrs. Marker Pepps could make of herself if the stock in her brother's ice-house should run short,—it struck him that two people could not be at loggerheads concerning such a little word as "out," unless it was a word that had various meanings for various people in various conditions. And when, on the retirement of the ladies, that individual had drawn an easy-chair up to the far-side of the fireplace, and was permitted— through Sir Topham entertaining the company with a lively narrative of his daily labours during the fort-

night he sat on the Committee for Inquiry into Turn-
pike Trusts,—a topic which Sir Topham illustrated
with the most diverting figures and unanswerable
statistics,—during this narrative, I say, the individual
before mentioned was permitted to enjoy the solace of
his own thoughts, and to come to the conclusion, that
the little word OUT was as full of changes as a pantomime ; and, that its three letters—even to a T—were
suggestive of many, and varied, scenes in our Life-
drama.

Let us glance at a few of them.

When Mr. Lamb said that his sisters were " out,"
he meant that they had been publicly introduced to
the society of their own neighbourhood, through the
medium of their County Ball.   But, when Mrs.
Marker Pepps asked the question, she looked above
county balls, and wished to know if the Misses Lamb
were " out," by having been introduced to society at
large, and Society *par excellence*, at the Court of Her
Most Gracious Majesty.   So that, here were two
different meanings to the word, although both meanings were designed to express one and the same thing.
And, descending in the scale of social rank, the word
would undergo still further change; for Miss Pounce,
the attorney's daughter, would be " out " when she
had appeared at their Town Ball; while Miss Plum,

the grocer's daughter, not aspiring to the Town Ball, would be "out" at the Tradesmen's Ball; and Miss Peach, the fruiterer's daughter, would be "out" as soon as she had made her appearance at the "jig," or a "grown-up party" of any kind.

Perhaps you don't know Mrs. Hurdle? one of the most good-natured of women, though more lavish of her hospitality than of her "h's," which she introduces into her conversation 'quite promiscous,' with an audacity that would send a thrill through Mrs. Marker Pepps' finely-toned mind. "Yes, Mister Jones," says Mrs. Hurdle; "we're a-going, as usual, to run down to Rhyll for a month's sea-siding. We *must* have our little Hout, you know; and its quite surprisin' 'ow it sets 'Urdle hup."

"What's the matter with you?" asks the doctor, as a patient comes groaning into his surgery; "have you hurt your arm?" "Yes, Sir!—Oh, law!—yes, Sir; it's the collar-bone, if you please, Sir! it's *out!*" Poor fellow! his is a painful experience of the meaning of the word.

Not half so agreeable, I dare wager, were his feelings regarding this little word, as were the sensations of my friend Jones, after Mr. Molar, the celebrated dentist, had been putting him to the most excruciating agony for half-an-hour, and had at length with-

P

drawn the offending **tooth,** saying, " There, Sir ! **it's**
out !" That little word insured for Jones a peaceful
application to his business, and a sound night's rest
after the **fatigues** of the day.

Do you know M'Cullum, of Cullum ? If so, you
will have heard, scores of times, those wearisome
anecdotes of his, commencing, " When my grand-
father was *out* in forty-five." Poor M'Cullum ! he
could **descant** on that little word " out," and tell you
how it brought him to his present condition (manager
of a country bank), instead of being the Laird **of**
broad Scottish acres, and of " brave Dunie-wassels **a**
thousand times three."

Talking of banks, I presume that it is not without
emotions of a pleasing nature, that the generality of
us **view the** word OUT on the swinging door of the
Bank, when we are going to draw a pretty heavy
cheque, and feel that we shall leave a strong balance
still **in our favour.**

When I called the other day on Mrs. Tomkins, and
inquired if she were at home, the footman unblush-
ingly replied, " Misses is *hout,* Sir ! " although I had
caught sight of **her** over the window-blind. Here,
the meaning of the word " out " would have to be
expressed by the periphrasis, " I don't wish to see you.
If you cannot come to my Twelfth-night party, when

you would have been really useful, you need not
trouble yourself to come here on other occasions.
Your place can be much better supplied by people of
greater consequence." So, I leave my card, and walk
away.

"Heard the news?" gasps old Puffy, as he hobbles
into his Club (the Megatherium). "Whawt noos?"
drawls little Dick Timmins. "Why, Ministers are
out!" "Bai Jove!" drawls Dick, with no more
enthusiasm than if he were the Duke of York's column hard by; while old Puffy, in a highly-explosive
state, like a worn-out locomotive, hobbles on, seeking
whom he may devour—anxious to find some one else
to whom he can impart the gratifying news. Ask my
Lord Grannydean, what is the meaning of "out" in
his Parliamentary sense. He would tell you that he
is *out* of place, *out* of pocket, and *out* of popular
opinion.

But, the servants of the Crown are not the only
people who are out of place;—though, indeed, we
might say of some Ministers, that they are quite *out*
of place in the offices they hold when *in* place. Domestic servants share the same fate. "Are you still
in service?" asks Mrs. Brown, when she casually
meets her daughter's former maid. "Ho no, mem,"
replies the late Miss Parker. 'Hive bin *hout*, mem,

some time, mem. My name's Binns now, mem. I married Binns, as you may call to mind, mem, was hone vally to the Hurl òf Button'ole. We keeps a greengrocer's business, mem. Binns 'ires 'imself out to wait on parties, and I gets up fine linen and clear-starching. Hallow me to 'and you one of our cards, mem !"

Very probably, if Mr. Binns is not going to assist at any high-life (or "au-ton," as he calls it) dinner party this evening, he will be found in the snug parlour of "The Polyphemus and Squint," at the weekly meeting of "The Gentlemen-of-the-Livery Club;" where, doubtless, he will favour his former companions of the plush with his celebrated song of "*Out* John !" And when, after a great consumption of tobacco and spirits-and-water, the most modest of the plush-wearers observes that it's a getting late, and asks Mr. Binns if he's a going 'ome ; that gentleman observes, with a slight haziness of articulation— "Goinome ! zatsa fine 'dea ! no ! sallstayere anzeit *out !*" What the "seeing it *out*" means, the late Miss Parker will discover when her liege lord is as-sisted to his residence in a state which forbids him employing himself otherwise than by snorting and sleeping.

When a schoolboy wishes to "choose sides" for

any game, and sets *out* his companions in a ring,
and points to each in turn, repeating the schoolboy
formula—

> " One-ry, two-ery, tickery teven ;
> Alabo, crackabo, ten and eleven ;
> Spin, spon, must be gone :
> Alabo, crackabo, twenty-one.
>   O-U-T spells *out !*"*

he little thinks he is repeating a form of words which
is said to have been handed down from the Druids,
and which is met with, under various changes, in all
parts of Great Britain, and, as Mr. Halliwell shows,
in Sweden also.

But, from youth to age, in all the ins and *outs* of
Life we find *out* our little word " out," figged *out*
in all kinds of dresses, and coming *out* among all
sorts of company.

When the day had at length arrived for that memorable Hazledean pic-nic, to which Fanny Gush had
been looking forward so anxiously, did she not, the
instant that she was awaked, spring *out* of bed, and
jump upon a chair to have a look at the old-fashioned
weather-prophet who stood on the top of the chest of
drawers, in the shape of a little house with a little man

* This formula is given by Mr. Halliwell, in his *Popular Rhymes*,
p. 134.   Many other versions of the formula are given in the tenth
volume of " Notes and Queries."

and woman vibrating *out* of its two little porticoes?
And did not Fanny clap her hands, and cry exultingly
to her sister, "Joy, joy! it will be a fine day, Nelly!
The old woman is *out !*" I am given to understand
that she *did* go through this *tableau vivant;* and
moreover—her animal spirits being unusually high—
that she concluded her **performance** by throwing her
pillow at her prostrate sister! And all this, because
the little old woman was not inside her portico, **but**
out.

But, talking of a lady in her *robe-de-nuit,*—I go to
see *Macbeth* murdered by that eminent tragedian Mr.
G. V. Snookes, and I hear the Lady Macbeth of the
night exclaim, "Out (*improper expression*) spot! *out,*
I say!" and she rubs her hands, and strides about in
her night-gown. Here "out" means, that "all great
Neptune's ocean" will not wash away that spot; and,
that "all the perfumes of Arabia will not sweeten that
little hand."

Who can forget the pictorial application of that
other Shakspearian *out*-line — "Out! out, brief
candle!"—that *Mr. Punch* so cleverly made to the
ex-(or *out*) King Louis Philippe? No one can forget
it, or those *out*-lines illustrative of " Yᵉ manners and
customes of yᵉ Englyshe" with which Mr. Doyle so
decked *out* **Mr. Punch's** picture-gallery.

But there are other *out*-lines to be seen. **Let us go** with Clive Newcome and his friend **J. J. to** Gandish's. It is the Life Class ; and a model, with an invaluable beard, is posed for the father in "Jephthah's Rash Vow." **The** red-haired Scotch student, Mr. **Sandy** McCollop, is hard at work at his drawing-board ; **and Mr.** Gandish looks over his **shoulder, and scans his** outline with a critical eye. "Your drawing is *out,* Sir !" he says ; and he points to the places : "here, Sir ; and here ; and here. **It is** altogether *out,* Sir." **So** a piece of bread is called into **requisition; and because** the *out*-line is *out,* it must **be rubbed** *out.*

I meet Tomkins at the Club, and I say to him, **"I** hear that Miss Plover's match with Jack Snipe is *off?*" "My dear feller !" says Tomkins, "you are altogether *out.*" By which **he** means, that I have become the depository of incorrect information, and that there is a probability of Miss Plover even now changing her name into that of Snipe.

As I leave the Club, and make **a sharp turn at the** corner of the street, against whom should I jostle, but that fire-eating individual Captain O'Trigger. "Bedad!" says the Captain after I have apologized, and assured him that the concussion was, on my part, quite accidental, "And it's fortenate for ye, Sir, that it was onintentional ; or it's satcesfaction I should have been after asking **ov ye." And I feel that** the Captain does not hold out the duel as an empty threat ; for it is well known that he has been *out* a sufficient number of times to enable him to keep his hand in practice, and to be (in slang language) " an Out-and-Outer."

O Mr. Felix-on-the-Bat ! describe to me, in your felicitous language, what must have been the sensations of Mr. Bale on that momentous day when he played in the celebrated match between the Twenty-two of Muggleton and its District, against the Eleven of England ! Recount how that illustrious amateur cricketer, after extensive and expensive practice under the tuition of a professional bowler,—after swiping threes, and even fours, in fevered dreams, amid the silent applause of shadowy spectators,—after making proud boast to envious friends of his deeds of batting fame,—after individually advising the Twenty-one Muggletonians how to block Mynn's shooters, and what to do with Clarke's sneaks, and Pilch's twisters, —recount, O Mr. Felix-on-the-Bat, how he took up his position at the wicket—a sight to see in his flannels, and paddings, and india-rubbers ! Tell the world, how he measured the ground, and patted it, and trod it, and held his bat knowingly up on end while he called " Give me block, Sir !"—relate, still further, how he took up his position in his very best attitude,—how the Muggletonians looked on with admiration and expectation, as the Umpire called " Play !"—as Mr. Pilch delivered

the ball—as Mr. Bale raised his bat to strike! and
then, if you have the power to grapple with so sad a
theme, communicate to the world the shame and
anguish of the Muggletonian champion on hearing a
noise among his stumps, and the voice of Mr. Box
the wicket-keeper, exclaiming " *Out !*"

" Fancy waft me in golden vision " to the side of
Miss Hannah Smithers, and her sister Maria. They
are seated on a music-ottoman; and are endeavouring
to strum the Tum-tum-titumtitee of Verdi's " Donna
è mobile," arranged as a duet. Miss Hannah waggles
her head to the tune; and Miss Maria—who takes
the treble—counts " One—two—and three and four !"
to mark the time. But the young ladies not having
much music in their souls, cannot run on very well
together. Miss Hannah jibs, and drops a note;
whereby the running accompaniment of her bass
comes into the melody at inopportune seasons; and
Miss Maria exclaims (somewhat testily), " Hannah !
you are *out !*"

When your wife goes to the Drapery and Shawl
Emporium of Messrs. Bobbinet and Co., and inquires
for some particular pattern of some new fashion, Mr.
Bobbinet rubs his hands, and smirkingly replies, " We
had a large stock of them last week, M'm; but there
was such a demand for them, that we can't procure

them fast enough ; and, just at present, we are quite *out* of the article. But allow me to show you, M'm, a sweet thing in shawls—the Sebastopol shawl. The pattern, as you observe, represents the capture of that 'uge fawtress. Chaste design, and just *out !*"

If you go to the circulating library, for Mrs. Slip-slop's new novel of fashionable life " The Magnolia of May Fair ; or, the Count and the Coronet," ten to one—(so great is the popular thirst for the Slip-slopian rill)—ten to one, but you will find that all the three hundred copies of the book are *out*.

A book, too, will be out of print; its author may have been out of money by it ; its publisher may have been out of pocket, and therefore out of temper, by it.

Just so,—Poke-bonnets are out of date ; oysters are out of season in June ; a hack is out of condition ; a race-horse is out of So-and-so by So-and-so; a house is out of repair ; a coat is out at elbows ; street-singing mechanics are out of work.

Friends fall out ; Ranters shout out ; babies roar out ; ministers go out ; young ladies come out ; noses are put out ; intrusive people are commanded to get out ; quarrelsome people are apt to fly out ; imperti-nent people are liable to be kicked out ; of their money, people run out.

Debutantes and new books will be brought out ;

measures and railway works will be carried out; fainting ladies and shop-fronts will be taken out; lecture-rooms and the dresses of corpulent people will be let out; nervous orators and actors will be ordered to speak out, or, in vulgar language, "to spit it out."

Colours may be washed out; purses may be cleaned out; patience may be worn out.

People will assemble on the last night of the Old Year, to see it out; schoolboys will enjoy a tuck-out, or a blow-out; bustling housekeepers will delight in having a good turn-out; cryers will give it out; dare-devils will face it out; story-tellers will brazen it out, until they are found out.

If you wish to rid yourself of a fault, you must root it out; if you wish to enlarge your dining-room, you must throw it out; if your premises are on fire, the engines will endeavour to put it out; if you wish to act as jackal to any literary lion, you must draw him out; if you wish to make the most of anything —a magazine article, for instance—you must spin it out.

I would say more, but my paper—like my subject —is   O U T !

THE WATER-LILY.

THE earth lay dreaming in a golden light;
   The tall trees cast their shadows in the pool
Where lay the Water-lily gleaming bright
   Amid the sedgy umbrage dun and cool.
All clad in purest white, like saintly nun,—
   Or like some veil'd bride,* in nuptial dress,
Who feels another's heart in her's is wound,
Another life—of Duty—is begun,
   And trembles in her love and loveliness,—
Amid its shining leaves it lay at rest,
Reclined upon the water's throbbing breast,
Answ'ring its every motion, every bound,
As though some mystic love to them was given:
The Vestal of the Wave, it lay and look'd to Heaven.

   * *Nymphœa* (νυμφη, "a bride ") *alba* is its botanical name.

OAK - FELLING AND BARKING.

A TREE that takes 200 years to arrive at its full growth
of 120 feet, surely demands a little notice when it is
cut down, even if it does not arouse our sympathetic
feelings to intercede for its life, and bid the " Woodman
spare the tree, and touch not a single bough," as was
the case with the lady in the song. And when we
reflect that this same tree will, in all probability, be
fashioned into the rib of some leviathan of the deep,
or be formed into the plank that separates the sailor
from death, we cannot look upon its removal from its
forest home or country sward, without feeling an interest in its fate far different to that with which we regard
the fall of an elm or an ash. There are materials for
thought and a suggestiveness of subject in the felling
of an oak, that could be turned to valuable account by
the poet; and as the poet and the painter are twin
spirits, the subject addresses itself as strongly to the
stainer of canvas as to the spoiler of paper. It has
received illustration from the powerful pencil of Lin-
nell, in a picture which is among those in the Vernon

Collection; and no landscape **artist has** passed over
the rugged grandeur and solid magnificence of "the
brave **old oak.**"   If Tennyson could so far forget the
respect due to its regal dignity as to say, in his " Am-
phion," that—

> " The *gouty* oak began to move,
>   And flounder into hornpipes"—

(a Royal *abandon* that surpasses the dancing of the
masquerading bluff King Hal at Cardinal Wolsey's
banquet)—yet he amply makes the *amende honorable*
in his " Life and Conversations" of that talking oak,
the glorious and **much-to-be-envied** "broad oak of
Sumner-chace," **whose** knotted knees were deep in fern,
and whose good fortune **it was to** be clasped and kissed,
and slept under, and have sonnets made on, by a
young lady who was as gamesome as a colt, and livelier
than a lark, and who, Dryad-like, was to wear on her
wedding morning a wreath

> " Alternate leaf and acorn-ball."

We are not prepared to state—as Cabinet Ministers say
when they want to shuffle out of a too-pressing question—whether or not the arboreal hero of our present
sketch was ever taken into the confidence of a similarly "gamesome" young lady.   If so, it was to be
envied.

But there it lies.   The antlered monarch of the

forest is laid **low : its** pleasant place **on** the gently-sloping hill **on the** woodside, shall know it no more. There is a gap **in** the landscape where it once stood so proudly, and the clustering fern and velvet grass shall **never again be** shrouded beneath its outstretched arms. Some of them have been already lopped **off,** and those that remain are doomed **to amputation.** There is the head physician, Dr. Woodman, with his upraised axe, who will cut off all those Briarean arms, as soon as his subordinates have stripped **away** the bark, and the monarch's once handsome form **will be reduced to a** shapeless trunk.

It is a busy scene, **this oak-barking,** and one in which young and old—man, **woman, and** child—can be actors. While the young and **active men** swarm into the branches, and take up perilous positions aloft, the old men, and even the women, can be thumping away below, loosening (with the back of the axe-head) the bark of detached branches, or of those arms of **the** tree which have been brought near **to** the ground ; while the children can find ample employment in the same occupation, or in piling into heaps **the** detatched pieces of bark. When there is a good staff of workers, who can industriously ply their barking-irons and peeling-irons (which **are** like large cheese-tasters), or their axe-heads, it is astonishing to see with what

rapidity a gnarled and rugged tree cau be converted
into a sleek and shining specimen, that looks something between satin-wood and ivory. By dint of a
little judicious thumping the rough exterior is quickly
exchanged for the polished surface—from which an
instructive moral may be drawn by those who teach
the ingenuous arts, and the young ideas—and the
peeling-iron is made to do its work with great efficiency,
as well as rapidity. Only the chief branches and arms
of the tree are left for this purpose; all the lesser
branches and twigs are bound up into "cords," with
the other loppings and chips, which are to the Woodman, what dripping and fat are to the cook—his
perquisites.

Oak-barking always makes a pretty scene. The
number and variety of the figures, and their diversities
of attire and posture, afford good material for the
artist, and amusement for the spectator. The tortuous
branches of the felled tree are, here and there, brown
with the yet-unremoved bark, and in other places
gleam white against the blue April sky. There are
the first spring flowers to enamel the grass and charm
the senses of sight and smell: the pale primrose and
the cloistered violet; the meadow crocus and the gentle
snowdrop; the golden kingcups and celandines; the
peeping cowslip-buds, Herrick's daffodils, and Burns's

daisies. The trees in the wood are putting forth their green shoots; **the lark is** singing high in the heavens; and butterflies are abroad in all their beauty. By the woodside they have stacked the lopped branches of the oaks that have been already felled; and against one of these stacks they have made a rude hut to smoke and **dine** in when the weather is wet. There is abundance of wood wherewith to keep the **fire** burning, and Tommy's cheeks and mouth form into a capital pair of bellows. A good wife has brought a provision basket, in which, no doubt, there **is a** " sup o' cider " or beer, in defiance of Father Mathew and Mr. George Cruikshank. When the bark has been stripped from the trees it will be **put into rows, sheltered** at the top, in order that it may be dried. This is called " ranking," and is a process that occupies about three weeks.

It will then be carted off, and set up into stacks, like wheatstacks, or, as is more commonly the case, will be at once taken off to its purchaser. At the oak-harvest season, quite a feature at that period of the year consists in the long lines of bark-laden waggons that may be seen wending their way to some neighbouring tanyard. Its bark thus being such a valuable commodity, and its wood being still more valuable, the oak comes to be looked upon in a monetary light by out-of-elbow squires, and needy noblemen, who **pay** their debts of honour by a cheque upon the bank of nature; and, when the dice and the turf have been unpropitious, repair their losses by an order to their steward, to fell some timber. Then are certain trees, which were old acquaintances of our great-great (ever-so-many-great!) grandfathers, doomed to destruction, and come out to the world ticketed with red numerals—rubrics that give directions for their own death. Then do the advertising columns of county newspapers proclaim that " Messrs. Hammer and Co. are instructed to offer for public competition four hundred superior old oak trees—a great proportion grove-oak of fine quality, large and lengthy, and suitable for navy timber." Then is this statement echoed from village barns and dead walls, by placards that are printed in letters of a size calculated to astonish, if not enlighten, the agricultural mind. Then do Messrs. Hammer and Co. sell the aforesaid four hundred superior old oak-trees, and do thereby make four hundred lacerations in the hearts of many lovers of nature and the picturesque. Then arrive whole armies of " fellers"—woodmen and barkers—who, for the next month, assault the ears of the neighbourhood with the reverberating strokes of the axe. And then may be seen those picturesque and noisy *tableaux vivants* of which we have here given a still-life representation.

LITERARY LADIES' PEN-MONEY.

THE education of women has attained to the assumption of excellence, if not to **excellence itself**. **Our** modern misses learn everything,—superficially, on the whole,—but their smattering of general knowledge gives them a greater **variety of** objects for thought, and opens up to them subjects from which their deductive intellects can derive suggestive **topics** for remark. Thus, their general intelligence is thereby raised, although they may not be able to talk learnedly, or correctly, on scientific subjects, or to fulfil the stringent regulations laid down for their guidance in social ethics by such over-wise teachers as Mrs. Ellis. Nor is it desirable that this hot-bed and palm-house system of education should be introduced into the flower and kitchen gardens of every-day life. **A man needs** for **his** wife a woman, and not a schoolmaster, or a doctor of divinity ; and the best education of a woman we take to be that which will train her for a loving wife, and not for an unsociable pedant. It will not, in the long run, make the husband an essentially happier man, because his wife is able to discuss with him the beauties of a chorus in *Sophocles,* or the usefulness of the solution of equations by approximation; nor will the fact that she is as well up in her classics as was Lady Jane Grey, or Mary Queen of Scots, necessarily ensure the domestic comfort of her husband, although, if he be an ordinarily intelligent man, he will be glad to have a wife whose intellect is sufficiently acute to enable her to take an interest that is not fictitious in the matters of science or learning that daily delight him. But, "true yoke-fellows!" will always be able to pull well together, whatever may be the fashion of their harness; and the thousand simple realities of daily life are far more common and important than a few classical contingencies and inconsidered trifles of scattered sciences.

Woman's power to please is a quality specially bestowed upon her; and she may evince it through the medium of her pen, much more than from the exercise of her skill over the strings of the piano and harp; for, with her pen, she can

> " fret the string,
> The master-chord of man's heart,"

and make its vibrations respond to every phase of feeling.

The enthusiasm that is so natural to woman must

find some vent. **It** has often to be repressed by the trammels of **society, or by** timidity, **or by lack of** opportunity; **for how,** for example, can a young **lady** talk with **meet** enthusiasm on the delights of reciprocal affection and **wedded bliss,** when she has no one **near her to** whom she **would care to make the** observation, and when there **is no one of** the other sex who has distinguished her by that marked preference which gives the key-note for such remarks? But, endow that young lady with the faculty of expressing her sentiments **coherently and connectedly, and** allow her to sit down, **pen in hand, in the privacy of her** own room, with the permitted privilege **of** giving the **reins to her** imagination and **fancy, and** then see how her enthusiasm will gush forth, and how her natural **thoughts and feelings will** be expressed. She can then lay aside bread-and-butter timidity and the repressing formulas of conventionality, and can make her fictitious Amelia prattle to her imagined Edwin all those pretty things that she herself would like to say if any **real Edwin would** unfetter **her** tongue; she **can provide lovers for** her friends; can make conversation for them; **can marry them, and bless them** with a fruitful crop of olive-branches; and can do all this **in a way which will give pleasure to** herself in the writing, and may extend that pleasure to others in the reading. And more than this—it will not be an expensive pleasure; for it may put money in her purse and endue her with well-earned fame; or, if not that, it will at any rate repay her by the healthy mental exercise with which she has refreshed her nature in the composition of her tale or poem. Anything is better than idleness and Berlin wool; and the young lady who, without neglecting home duties and the demands of her family and station in life, has occupied a portion of her leisure time by strengthening her mind with a self-imposed task that will call out her best faculties, and force upon her something like systematic reflection and sustained exertion, has surely achieved something with which she may be reasonably satisfied, although her performance may not be destined for printer's ink,—or, if it be, may not rise to a higher position than to fill a nook in the corner of the local newspaper, or a few pages of an Eleemosynary Magazine supported by voluntary contributions.

But, perhaps, she has been successful with her literary labours; and, if she is able to keep them up after her marriage—instead of laying them aside, together with her other "accomplishments"—then, however dowerless she may have been, yet, out of the intellectual poetry of her nature, she will be enabled to bring towards the house-keeping her own share of that which is necessary for **the** prosaic sustenance of home. **In this case, her own** pen-money will be of more real worth than any pin-money received from her husband; and we can imagine few more sincere pleasures than would be felt by a young **wife—devoted not so much** to literature as **to** the interests of her husband and family—when she reflects that the cloth-**ing** of herself and children has been purchased with the proceeds of her own pen-money,—or, that the **ex**-penses of the trip to the sea-side which conferred so great a **benefit on** her over-tasked husband were de-frayed by the same means. *Bonnet* rhymes with *son-net;* **and, when** the former has **been** procured with the price of the **latter, the wearer may** be permitted to indulge in **a** little harmless vanity. Not that we would desire that our modern misses should be so educated that each one should be enabled (like a cooped fowl) to support herself out of the proceeds of her pen; or that they should be condemned to lead a spider-like existence by **spinning the** means **for** sustenance **out of** their **own brains. No!** the **whole duty of woman** is **not to write poems, but to live** them **; nor even is** it obligatory **upon spinsters** to spin any other works than those which may be adapted to household **purposes, or personal use.** Yet, as **a** bird that *can* sing and won't sing, ought to be made to sing, so ought a woman of literary tendencies to cultivate her intellect, and make it subservient to good and useful ends. If she gain nothing more than the self-culture and self-discipline to which her task will give rise, she will have obtained an ample reward for her industry and painstaking; but there is no reason which should prevent her from endeavouring at the same time to earn a little pen-money. The poetry of life is not for every one, while its prose is for all; but when lyrics can be exchanged for legs of mutton, there is a happy meeting of sentiment and reality, which is the most gratifying instance of free-trade reciprocity that housekeeping experience can afford. It may be very prosaic to take this view of the advantages to be derived from the pursuits of literature; but, at any rate, the practical and poetical can each have its turn, and both are within the scope of Literary Ladies' Pen-money.

THE HERO AND THE MAIDEN.

[The following lines were written for the late Lady Victoria
T——, in commemoration of her visit to the 'Gallery of Illustration'
in company with the late Duke of Wellington, who presented to
her a Book descriptive of 'The Wellington Campaigns,' in which
he had written some lines as a *souvenir* of their visit. May 10, 1852.
The duke died on September 16, of the same year.]

A maiden, in her summer pride—
   A warrior, on whose reverent head
   The wintry snow of Time is spread,
In a dusk room sit side by side.

The maiden comes of high degree,
   And bears a name as noble; one
   That ever went with Wellington—
Victoria, and Victory!

A burst of light, and lo! a mass
   Of scenes, whose names have lived for long
   In hist'ry's page and poets' song,
In pictured shape before them pass.

Q

New are the scenes to her; but not
  To him whose prowess gave renown
  To mountain-pass and country-town,
And household words made every spot;

Where, with a valour like his own,
  His conquering legions, far and wide,
  Dash'd on in one triumphant tide,
And swept Napoleon from his throne.

Roll on the record! bring to view
  The fields of fight that won him fame,
  And crown'd him with a deathless name,
Won from the world at Waterloo!

So let them pass! the painter's art
  O'er realms of fancy may prevail;
  But here, the magic wand must fail,
That bids *such* scenes to being start.

The mimic shapes must feebly paint
  The bloodstain'd battle's deep, dark dye,
  And seem, to *his* far-piercing eye,
But shifting shadows, dim and faint;

But shifting shades, that come and go
  Over clear memory's sunlit field,
  The shades of giant strifes that seal'd
The fate of nations with a blow.

And what **thinks he, whose outward calm**
 Betrays **no throb of** passion's tide,
 The **warrior of the world! whose** pride
Was but to gain the peaceful palm?

Unmoved he seems by all; and—save
 When some few kindly **words he speaks,**
 And **thus the charméd stillness** breaks—
Sits stern and silent as the grave.

Yet great thoughts *must* be **his; and she—**
 The maid of twenty **summers—knows**
 How full must be the stream that flows
From such a fount of Memory.

And she, until her death, will **hold**
 The recollection of that hour
 As **proudest of the** thoughts **that dower**
A heart **that loves the** Brave and **Bold.**

And that small book **shall rise to** worth
 All priceless—yea, an **heirloom proud—**
 The gift of one whom all avow'd
The greatest General e'er **on** earth.

 . . . . . .

Four fated months had spun their thread
 Of mingling colours, dark and fair;
 The roll of battles still was there—
Their **Hero** slept beside the dead!

9 7 8 3 3 3 7 0 7 5 6 4 4